EVERYDAY MENTORING

Cover design by Kinsey Schick

Edited by Holly Lomelino, Claire Albrecht & Jonathan Madajian

Formatted by Abigail Benton

ISBN: 9798876441133
Imprint: Independently published.

Printed in the United States of America

For further resources, please visit
everyday-mentoring.com

TABLE OF CONTENTS

INTRO

This book is the result of over twenty years of walking with God. It is a crown of wisdom that has been forged in the furnace of relationship. When I was younger, back when God and I were still in our honeymoon phase, I asked one of my mentors for advice about where I should study for seminary. His response cleared away a bit of brush along my life's path: "Biblically, nobody went to seminary. They simply got married and started a family." The implication of this simple statement was that family is where we learn to love. Family is the training ground where we grow in being more concerned with others than we are with ourselves.

Looking back from where I am now, I guess you can say that I took this advice very seriously: I have been married for twenty-one years and I have seven kids ranging from eighteen months old to eighteen years old at the time of writing this book. Family is everything to me. Family is where I have learned the most about myself, the world, and God. Family is also where I have explored different ways of thinking, being, and doing before distilling information to our church family and the world. I like to say that if it doesn't work in my home, then the last thing I want to do is bring it to the public.

Something I have learned is that life can be based around many things; however, a strong case can be made that the best focal point is relationship. If you recall some of the most memorable moments of your life, the most joyful or most sacred or most intentional, the odds are that they are connected to people. I believe this is because God has designed us to be connected to others as well as God directly. Despite being designed for connection, many people struggle to live connected lives and the most common reason I see for this is an unhealthy inner world.
Making a commitment to developing a healthy inner life is one of the most important things we can do with our lives, but it will also be one of the hardest commitments to live out. The first piece of advice I would like to offer in this book is this: keep your heart tender and teachable. The only way we can avoid growing calloused and jaded is by committing ourselves to learning and listening as we go through the journey of life. We must stay humble before God and be willing to learn from the world around us.

As I have continued my walk on the path of life, I have noticed that the most wise and happy and impactful people often live simple lives. That is why I have worked to make this book as short and to the point as possible. It is inspired by the Proverbs: simple truths that can be easily applied to our lives.

That being said, no matter how practical I make this book, the biggest rewards will come from applying what is taught. Before you begin reading through this book, I encourage each of you to begin expecting to experience new views and ideas for living. Be curious. Take notes. Pray through what you read. Put into practice what is highlighted. Without application, this will just become another book you read but down the road you will be unable to remember what spoke to you.

BEFORE WE BEGIN

The greatest enemy to growth in this time will be distraction. We all are faced with outside pressures asking for our time and attention. Modern technology always has a notification, an answer to a momentary question, or a glimpse into a life that is "better" than yours. All of these distractions take place in the outside world, but as we mentioned earlier, this commitment is to shaping the inside world: to cultivating peace within us so that it can be brought into the world around us. Jesus reminds us that there is a path that leads to life even though few decide to walk on it. Let us not forget that we have what it takes to find it and we are never alone in this journey. I hope and pray that we are able to find this path during our time together.

Lastly, I would love to offer a pastoral reminder: life is much bigger than each of us. This is why our church family has opted for the phrase "all fruit is family fruit." This means that my win is your win and your win is my win. The growth that we have in God and the ways that we choose to face each day has a direct impact on the type of world we create; there is no such thing as a neutral life. I am praying that this book provides you with new tools, or sharpens tools you have, for living with eternity in sight. I am praying that we all live for the glory of God and the the good of those around us. I am praying that each of us would step into the life God created us to live and wake up with joyful expectation of all God wants to do through the one life that we get to live.

Onward & Upward,
Jason Lomelino

everyday-mentoring.com

CHAPTER 1: NOT LIVING FOR MYSELF

I want to start us off here in the deeper end of the pool because this is a principle that has the power to radically shift how you experience life. I will say that it is one of the most challenging things we can do (not living for ourselves); however, it is also one of the most rewarding ways we can live. As we go through this chapter, I invite you to consider what God is speaking to you and how God may be inviting you to shift some parts of your life. Before we jump in, I want to give a brief word about how to read this book.

This book is meant to be interacted with the same way you would with a friend at a coffee shop: gently, friendly, and conversationally. I am here to provide wisdom I have gathered from my life and present it to you for your consideration. I am going to share some thoughts with you, and you are welcome to take them or leave them as you see fit. That being said, if something stands out to you, I would encourage you to take it seriously as you continue on your journey of life with God. All of life is a continuous invitation to widen our perspective as we stay open to what the Holy Spirit is saying to us. So here we go…

Please read this quote a few times before moving on:

"Waking up each day for 'me' and not for the glory of God and the good of others is at the root of almost all my problems."

I know that this language is strong. I'm sure some of you have an inner lawyer that is screaming out "I OBJECT" or at least questioning the validity of the statement. Please, if you can, take this time to consider what is being said.

Now, I know that it can be hard to believe that many of our problems come from a life where 'self' is at the center. If you are single, it is often much easier to get away with a life where we are the focus because in some ways you are. When you get married, however, the challenges of living this way are exposed. Then, if children come into the picture, you will be faced with a twenty-four-seven mirror that will give you twenty-twenty vision for how your life is actually impacting the people around you.

The truth is that waking up for oneself actually goes against our design. We are created by Love and for Love; hence, we are off when we hinder the flow of love in our life. A hose with a kink can still give out a little water, but once the kink is undone, the flow is much stronger: we are no different. As children of God, we are created to be a pipeline for the love of God to be seen and felt on earth. The way I see it, waking up for oneself simply leaves us frustrated, tired, and often alone. Genuine freedom comes when we recognize that at the root of many challenges we find that we are more focused on 'me' than on God or others.

God created humanity to be the image of God, the representatives of what God looks like. What does that mean exactly? Well, it means that as we continue to get to know God, our thoughts and desires and actions start to look a lot more like God's thoughts and desires and actions. When God chose to describe His own character, He decided that "love" was one of the best descriptors. As those made in the image of God, we are made to receive and give love because that is who God is.

Love is learned over a lifetime. It is not a skill we

master, but a person we become. We are learning to be like our Father, not by trying harder, but by being with Him: spending time in His presence, learning His heart, and slowly gaining His thoughts about our life and the people in it. I like how Paul puts it in Ephesians 5 when he says: "Watch what God does, and then you do it, like children who learn proper behavior from their parents. Mostly what God does is love you. Keep company with Him and learn a life of love. Observe how Christ loved us. His love was not cautious but extravagant. He didn't love in order to get something from us but to give everything of Himself to us. Love like that."

In 2001, I was radically arrested by the love of God in a church service. I walked into the building unchurched, up to no good, and set on a path to pursue the American dream. I did not leave that service the same way that I walked in. During that service, I experienced the presence of God like a wave of liquid love and peace. Pre-Jesus I had experimented with a few drugs, but I had never had an experience like this. I used drugs as a way to escape, but this met me where I was. I felt like I was ambushed, caught completely off guard by this encounter.

In the middle of this, I heard a voice clear as day ask me this question:

"Jason, what are you living for?"

This question shook me so hard that it toppled the future I had constructed for myself. I knew that the answer to the question was me and I knew that I could not continue living that way anymore. Jesus invited me to live a life free of living for myself; which, though unaware, was the good-est 'good news' I could have ever heard. After the love of God met me, I had a new vision for life based around the person and the mission of Jesus. I didn't even want to live life with myself at the center anymore, being the main character in the story, the experience of God was just too powerful. I had been invited by the tangible love of God to start living for the glory of God and the good of others.

To this day, I still struggle with selfish thoughts and desires; however, there is no question when it comes to the meaning of life. I know that finding my life means learning to lay it down each day. I know that the path to real freedom and joy is connected to a new mindset of crowning Jesus king and considering other people more important than myself.

FREEDOM IS UPWARD

Consider for a moment the times when you have felt most alive.

For many of us, these moments are when we find ourselves "about our Father's business" and showing up for the people that God has put around us. I cannot say this enough: the way to true freedom is not inward but upward.

I am going to say this one more time and invite you to really consider this:

The way to true freedom is not inward but upward.

I am all for healing and improving the systems in our lives (I wrote an entire book on living emotionally healthy called *A Life That Wins*). I strongly believe that God is present as we sort through unhealthy stuff from our past to make sure it does not show up in our present. I believe that God gets excited when we work on achieving greater levels of health in our life. That being said, I have yet to meet someone who is living free to love God and others who still has their lens focused on themselves.

Something I often say is "God is the goal of life." I don't believe that waking up with the goal to love everyone will make us into loving people. In fact, I actually believe that it will make us cranky and a not-so-fun person to be around. When we purpose to love people, before loving God, we are putting the cart before the horse, trying to spontaneously produce love within ourselves instead of having it flow through us from the source of Love.

Like the sun with heat, love will always beget love.

Keeping the Main Thing the main thing is essential to run the race with endurance. Paul told the church in Corinth that he was concerned that their minds were drifting from a simplicity and purity of devotion to Jesus. Keeping our gaze and affection on God will be our forever battle in this life.

A FOCUSED LIFE

When I think of the people who have been most impactful in the world, they are God-focused, God-saturated, and God-adoring: Paul the Apostle, Mother Theresa, and George Muller being a few of my favorites. Their first priority was God — His name, His story, and His life having their attention and being exalted. They were not worried about what others thought of them. They were not worried about themselves. Their gaze was first upward, then inward. This is the kind of life that changes us from the inside out, impacting everyone around us each day too.

When God isn't our vision for living, we wake up each day to live a fragile life — allowing people to both make us and break us. We find ourselves trying to get from people what we should be getting from God. Let's be clear: God will put people into our lives to help us grow and mature, but if anyone besides Him is our source, it's only a matter of time before the foundation we built begins to crumble.

DEALING WITH SELFISHNESS

I'll be honest with you, I rarely wake up with my first to-do being 'live for the glory of God and the good of others.' It would be very helpful, considering the fact that I currently wake up to eight other humans and three dogs — not to mention the people involved in our local church.

This is why creating a daily rhythm that allows me to put my focus on God and remind myself I am not the main character has been so instrumental in creating sustainability in my life.

Over the years, my rhythm has changed due to what was beneficial in the season I was in. In one season, there was a time when I would wake up each day and the first thing I would do is kneel in the quiet until my heart connected with God. Only after I had felt that connection would I begin to quietly and internally adore God and give God the authority over my day. To this day, I have found that the more often I take these intentional pauses, the easier I find it to hear the gentle reminders from God through my day, helping me to be more aware of Him and the needs of others.

I want to preface this next story by saying that I do not recommend you do this. During a previous season, I was finding myself overwhelmed by my own selfishness. In an effort to nip this selfishness in the bud, I was intentionally pausing three times each day to kneel before God and bring my heart into awareness of my union with Him. I used my phone to set reminders so that I could pause throughout the day at fixed times. One time, this alarm went off while I was in the middle of Target, so I dropped to my knees, lifted my hands, and began to thank God for all He had done in my life. I instantly felt freedom from my bondage to self.

I say this not because I think each of you should kneel down in the middle of your nearest department store, but to illustrate a point: sometimes spiritual breakthrough is preceded by physical acts. Our feelings can oftentimes follow our actions. And sometimes our feelings don't change until our actions change.

Selfishness is simple: people who are selfish are people who are overly concerned with themselves. When our life is spent meditating on our own image, whether it is our looks, our feelings, or how others perceive us, we slowly become more selfish. This places us in opposition to our design, which is to be people of Love. I have found that true joy is found when we are able to switch our focus away from us and toward God, to be more God-conscious than self-conscious.

Parenting has revealed more than anything else what it truly means to be selfless. To be a parent means your life is constantly interrupted. When you are parenting, there is minimal to no thankfulness, especially with young children. When you are parenting, there is no pay, in fact you are paying to be selfless haha! I think this may be part of God's design to help form us into the image of Jesus. That being said, you don't need to be raising children in order to shift your focus away from yourself, though you may need to be intentional about finding places to invest into others or take care of a puppy for a season.

TAKING ACTION

Selflessness can be cultivated by intentionally spending time each week with those who are less fortunate than you. This provides an opportunity to get out of your own head or staring at your own face instead of someone else's. This can be done with a local houseless shelter, or even with someone that you see around your community. The key is to show up with zero expectation of what can be given back to you and set your focus on loving whoever is in front of you. For years, I served at the Rescue Mission as a mentor to men in the program. The funny thing is, I was only a few years old in the Lord and had many areas that needed growth. It would have been easy to discredit myself and turn my life inward until I felt healthy enough to help someone else. Looking back, I am glad I didn't. I have a twenty year friendship with one man that I met in the program — he considers me his most loyal friend, even though our relationship is only through the phone these days as he is serving a twenty year prison sentence.

If you are hitting a wall, you may need to change your direction. I have seen it over and over again through my own life and the lives I have mentored: true freedom comes to those who shift their focus away from themselves and towards the people who are around them. This can be challenging, especially if we have well-worn habits of self-focus, but this is one of the beautiful parts of Jesus's leadership in our lives. He has better paths, ways, and desires in store for us if we will trust His leadership. The Bible says that we have not because we ask not.[1] Sometimes it is as simple as asking God for His thoughts, heart, and ways - then following what we learn. The road to freedom is often a road we wouldn't take without Him inviting us onto it.

HOW TO AVOID THE JESUS DRIFT

Hopefully we can all agree that this world doesn't look exactly like Heaven. In fact, the culture of this world is always trying to form us in ways that are contrary to the culture that Jesus came to establish (this is what Jesus called the "kingdom of heaven" or "kingdom of God"). This is why Jesus invited us to partner with Him and pray that God's "kingdom would come" and "His will would be done." However, if we are not paying close attention, we can be tricked into believing the cultural message that we should have what we want, when we want, how we want it. Despite the shiny exterior, this belief bears some nasty fruit. When we live like this, we actually are moving against the culture that Jesus established and taking life into our own hands instead of inviting God into building it together.

At our church I spend a good amount of time talking about what I call "Jesus-drift." Jesus-drift is the slow process from being focused on Jesus to being focused on other things. This happens when we are consciously, or more often unconsciously, spending time with someone or something else other than Jesus in our pursuit of happiness and satisfaction. We spend time trying to find what exactly will bring us the MOST purpose, the MOST excitement, the MOST happiness, when Jesus already promised us a path to a satisfied and purposeful life: Himself.

When we try to construct a life apart from Jesus, we are living in a sandcastle. Sandcastles are the unstable structures we live in and it is only a matter of time before the tide comes and disrupts those structures we have spent our life building. When this happens, the ripple affect can be devastating. Both for our own life, and the lives around us.

Even as believers, I think it can be very easy to forget that Jesus was a genius when it comes to understanding the world. I mean, come on. Jesus literally designed it, I am sure that He understands how it works. Not only this, but Jesus says that He came to give us all life that is robust and robust to the fullest.[2] Jesus invites us into the same joy and satisfaction that the Father, Spirit, and Son have had since before the beginning of time. The sacred circle has been opened for us to be a part and partake in that same fellowship that has existed amongst the Godhead for all eternity.

May we never forget this as well: God is pro-fun, pro-pleasure, and all about our happiness. When God created humans, they were placed in Eden. Eden literally translates to "pleasure." Our original design was to be in a "garden of pleasure," enjoying our union with God and the world that He made. We were made to enjoy life, one another, and the work that we do. This means that even when we hear Jesus say things about "losing our life to find it," we can trust that we are being invited into a better way of living. This is an invitation to freedom from self-centered living into a vast and fulfilling life in God.

TRUTH SETS US FREE

Here's the kicker: until I am free from me, it is almost impossible for me to love you.

Why?

Well, this is because part of me is still in it for what I can get rather than what I can give. I am by nature self-focused, which means that unless I am free from that focus, I will be using you instead of serving you.

When we think about what a healthy life in God looks like, we must take an honest assessment of our relationship with God and which kingdom we are building. In order to figure this out, we must ask ourselves a difficult question:

Am I open to God's correction?[3]

God is amazing at course correcting. The tricky part is that many of us move too quickly to hear the gentle invitations into God-focused ways of living. Sometimes this comes internally through the nudge of God's Spirit, sometimes this comes through people that God has put around us. The key to hearing these messages is being humble and tenderhearted enough to slow down and listen.

I opened this chapter with a statement: Waking up each day for 'me' and not for the glory of God and the good of others is at the root of almost all my problems. My goal in writing this chapter was not to convince you, but to give you some food for thought as you go through life. These are ideas that can be chewed on and thought through as you head on your journey through life. It is an invitation to consider that maybe some of our relational issues and frustrations have more to do with us than we thought. To wake up for the glory of God and the good of others is a lesson learned over a lifetime, a lesson we learn from watching Jesus and living by the Spirit. We will not arrive one day. Rather, each day, in fact each moment, we can choose to yield ourselves to God and grow in love for those around us.

CHAPTER 1 REFLECTION QUESTIONS

1. What stood out to you most from this chapter? Why do you think that is? How could you apply this?

2. What is your current life vision? In what ways does your vision align with God's Kingdom? In what ways do you feel it differs from God's Kingdom? How could you bring your vision into greater alignment with God's Kingdom?

3. Do you currently feel that you are open to correction from God? Why do you think this is?

CHAPTER 2: THE ULTIMATE LIFE HACK

If you have been in church for awhile, then you may have heard that the Spirit of God lives inside you. What this means is that because of what Jesus did on the cross, we have complete access to God, and that when we invite God into our lives, God is pleased to be a part of them. God can give us advice and wisdom, change the way we think, and change our lives. That being said, if you have been around church enough, then you may take the access that you have for granted.

Living life by the Holy Spirit is the ultimate life hack. Living this way is the difference between a black-and-white life and a world that is in full color. It is the difference between figuring everything out on your own, or figuring everything out with the Creator of all things. This is a Creator who loves and cares about you, who is excited to make decisions with you. Take a minute and reflect on this:

You have 100% access to God 100% of the time.

The Holy Spirit is the one who makes all things possible and empowers us to live out who we really are. The realization that the God who created everything, both seen and unseen, has invited each of us into knowing what He is like is radically good news. Each moment of each day is overflowing with opportunities to hear what God is thinking and speaking. There is nothing in all of creation that can cut off the voice of God from our lives.

God is always speaking; however, at times it can be difficult for us to hear what God is saying. Sometimes we believe lies about the nature of God that sabotage our trust. Sometimes we tell ourselves stories about the difficulty in hearing from God. This is why making intentional time to cultivate our connection with God and His voice has a way of turning up the volume: it makes it much easier to hear God's voice, to recognize the gentle tone of Love, and to listen to that voice of our Shepherd as He leads us on this journey of life.

LIFE HACK

Living life by the Holy Spirit is the ultimate life hack.

Jesus promised us that the Holy Spirit would guide us, lead us, teach us, comfort us, counsel us, and never leave us. The million dollar question is this:

Do we believe this?

Do we really believe what Jesus said, alongside John and the other apostles, that we do not need anyone to teach us because the Holy Spirit will teach us all things?[1]

To clarify, I am not advocating for being unteachable. I am writing this book as a way to encourage more health in God. However, I can't throw away what is clearly presented in the Gospel and the book of Acts: a radical life that is guided by the Holy Spirit. Consider for a second that the early church didn't have New Testament Scripture. The first "Christians," which means "little Christ," didn't follow writings: they followed a voice.

Now, the Scriptures are a gift and I don't believe that the Holy Spirit will ever contradict them. However, we must be careful that we do not rely on Scripture as the only way to hear God's voice. For me, the Bible has always been a springboard into the presence of God. A precious gift to know

God and understand how God intended life to work. I agree strongly with Timothy that Scripture was brought into the world by the Holy Spirit's guidance and that it has many uses for correcting and guiding us through life.[2]

John beautifully reminded us that in the beginning was the Word, and that this Word was with God and was God. In plain language, Jesus is the Word of God. The best part about this is that Jesus still speaks as clearly today as Jesus did before the beginning of time. The Bible is a beautiful on-ramp into communion with God. The Bible is a great place for finding wisdom, truth, correction, and insight. The Bible, or the written word, is also meant to point us toward Jesus, who is the living Word. The Bible is a tool that has been given to us so that we can experience deeper intimacy with Jesus and the union we have with God because of the Holy Spirit. Not to mention, I have found that cultivating relationship with God through the Word of God has made hearing God outside of reading Scripture so much easier too.

CONVERSATIONAL INTIMACY

In my experience, it seems that most people did not grow up in homes where conversation about life was easy to have. It appears to be rare that families have non-judgmental back-and-forth conversation about how to get wisdom and live emotionally healthy. This is why being welcomed into the family of God means getting new perspective on family dynamics. In this new family of Father, Son, and Holly Spirit we are safe, seen, heard, and allowed to ask for help whenever we need it.

Our God is communicative. It says in Psalms 139 that God is intimate and familiar with all our ways.[3] God delights to be involved in His children's lives. Back-and-forth conversation with God is our new normal, our birthright as sons and daughters of God. Unlike some of our parents, our God loves to be involved in the lives of His kids, to do life with them, and communicate His heart and thoughts to them.

I like the term "conversational intimacy," referring to the fact that we can talk to God and that God will talk back to us. We were created to hear God's voice. Think back to the creation story, where we see Adam (which translates "human" or "humanity") and Eve (which means "living") spending time listening, living, and working alongside God. In the beginning, face-to-face was the default, and taking walks with God was the way of life.

I grew up unchurched, which means I didn't have anybody tell me anything when it came to hearing God's voice in my life. Nobody told me "God doesn't speak today" or "miracles are a thing of the past." When I had my encounter with God over two decades ago and began to read the New Testament, I met a communicative God who did extraordinary things through ordinary people like me.

I remember one time, early on in my relationship with Jesus, when God asked me to pray for a woman that I didn't know. It turned out that she was going into surgery the next day to have gallstones removed. I didn't know who she was, but I did know the "Great Physician," so I did exactly what the doctor ordered. The next day, when this woman went to her scheduled appointment, the medical team was baffled because they couldn't find anything wrong with her. Jesus healed that woman just like I had read in the Gospels and Acts.

I have chosen to live my twenty plus years with God listening to God's voice in my life. I can't say that I always take full advantage of the access that we have nor the help that God wants to provide me each day, but I do place a high value on making time to listen to Him as a way of life. I can't even imagine what my life would be like today if I did not have the voice of God affirming, correcting, and guiding me into truth that sets me free.

God has saved me from so many dumb decisions. There have been countless times when God has spoken into a situation or a decision that I needed to make and given me insight that I would not have had otherwise.

I see this oftentimes with counseling. There are many times that I sit down with someone, ready to share what I think they need, only to hear the voice of God gently tell me "sssshhh, just listen." This is always followed by a much healthier conversation than it would have been in my "wisdom." The access we have to God's wisdom, thoughts, and way of life are available at all times if we want them. God is generous and loves to be involved, the key is invitation: asking God for His thoughts and what He thinks you should do.

When it comes to the voice of God, we want to think like a child. We want to live like sons and daughters: always asking questions and always eager to hear what mom & dad are saying. I am moved by King David, who before the cross or the gift of the Holy Spirit were given, knew God in a profound way. When we read the Psalms, which are like David's journal entries, we see a man who would not settle for a distant God. David wanted to know God and to be known by God. David wasn't afraid to share his heart or to ask God the big questions about life. This is what is available to us. Like David, we can have real conversations with God about our lives. We can also have a real trust that God listens to us and responds to us. God is excited for us to live in wisdom and health, we simply need to ask.

LISTENING PRAYER

Listening prayer is a game changer when it comes to knowing God. In any relationship, we need to slow down and enjoy the presence of the other person. Listening prayer is learning to linger with God. It is applying Psalms 46:10 and learning to "be still and know that [God] is God." As we learn to listen, we slowly learn to live in tune with the gentle song of the Holy Spirit.

Learning to listen is a journey with no destination. Rather, it is a meandering path through which we are able to explore various sights and sounds, soaking in the beauty. In more concrete terms, I am saying that when we practice listening prayer, we are focusing on being with God: seeing, hearing, and feeling what God invites us to see, hear, and feel. The practice is simple. We sit in a quiet place that is free of distraction and we turn our attention towards God. It is in giving our focus that we are able to have our souls restored.

I believe something mystical happens when we live a life of stillness. I can't think of a more helpful way to know God than spending time alone with Him in the quiet. It is possible to meet with God at a coffee shop or a church or a park, but there is something special that happens when we make space to be with God one-on-one. No noise. No distraction. No agenda. In this environment, we are able to lay down our root system, which in turn creates the structure for a fruitful life.

I like to say, "If it is good enough for Jesus, it is good enough for me." What I mean is that if Jesus needed something, like baptism or quiet places to be with God, then I probably need it too. When I look at Jesus' life, I see that He is constantly making space to hang out with God. I would even go so far as to say that this was the "secret sauce" of His life: Jesus spent time alone getting to know His Father.

THE VOICE OF GOD

Learning to hear the voice of God is something that gets easier the more we understand what God's voice sounds like. Listening prayer is one way that we start to recognize God's tone of voice, but there are many other ways that can grow this muscle. Asking God questions and journaling back the responses is another way that I have seen a lot of fruit, as well as inviting mature believers to help me discern what God is saying in a season. The key to growing the muscle is to exercise it.

The good news is this: the more that we work this muscle in private, the easier it becomes to use it in public.

Our church has a ministry known as Jesus Burgers that has been going on since 2001. Jesus Burgers has a house on the most popular party street in our city; there are seven girls living in the top unit and seven guys living in the bottom unit. On Friday nights, the residents of the house cook up and serve over two hundred burgers for anyone who wants them. For us, it is a practical way that we can love the city we live in, one burger at a time.

I remember one time at Jesus Burgers there was a girl waiting in line who was freaking out after losing a ring that her Grandma had given her. She was convinced that she had walked onto the property with the ring; however, I could tell she may have had a little too much to drink and I was skeptical of the story. Despite the skepticism, I told her that I would help look for it. I decided to ask God to tell me where the ring was. I instantly felt like it was under our picnic bench, which was strange because she was nowhere near that part of our property. I decided to check it out and sure enough, there was the ring! I immediately thought, "Yes, Lord!" and went to return it to the girl. She was so excited it was found, and it was so special to share how I knew where to look. She asked more questions about God when she saw that He cared about the same things she did. Never forget: learning to live by the voice of God is the path to a life of loving others well. Hearing God is truly the ultimate life hack in all areas of life.

THE JOURNEY

As we go on this journey together, please know that there is no habit, rhythm, or routine that can sustain more fruit in your life than living with attention to the voice of God. I have story after story of times I have tried to achieve outcomes my way, facing obstacle after obstacle, only to find out God had a much simpler path for me to walk on. Learning to cultivate a slower pace of life will take time, but it is nothing compared to the setbacks we put in our own way when we try to live apart from God. God deeply loves us and cares about us. Learning to build a life that asks God for wisdom and guidance is one of the foundational building blocks for a healthy, joyful, and empowering life with God and walking in the purposes of God.

CHAPTER 2 REFLECTION QUESTIONS

1. What stood out to you most from this chapter? Why do you think that is? How could you apply this?

2. Do you find it challenging or easy to tune into the voice of God? Why do you think that is?

3. How could you make more space to listen for God's voice in your life?

CHAPTER 3: RHYTHMS & ROUTINES

I want to start this chapter out with a truth I have seen in both my life and the lives of others I have mentored:

There is no health without rhythm.

A life without rhythm and routine is like a ship that is tossed to-and-fro by the many unpredictable waves of life. An intentional routine is the anchor: when conditions become uncertain and difficult to navigate, the anchor keeps us from drifting off course. Having an anchor is what keeps us tethered to our vision; it helps us remember what is important in life.

God was intentional in the creation of the world and He knows the way that it operates best. Humans are the pinnacle of creation and God put care into each one of us, knowing exactly what helps us to operate best. Over and over again as I have walked alongside people, I see that the more we can discover and live within the rhythms that uniquely suit us, the easier that our lives become.

Modern research is currently finding that ninety percent of our actions take place at the unconscious level. That is nuts!

We are spending most of our lives on autopilot.

Think about driving a car. When you first learned, you were hyperaware of all the things that you needed to do. Maybe you were too touchy on the brake or gas, you can't forget the blinker, not to mention you had to pay attention to where you were going. Though, after a while, with enough familiarity and practice, you are now able to make entire trips without even thinking about your driving. You are now able to do something which once took extreme focus with very little conscious effort.

Now, think about your favorite local coffee shop. Think about how often you order the same drink. Think about how often you sit in the same seat. This ability to operate without expending energy is a gift from God to help us live healthier lives; however, this gift can also turn into a curse if we are not intentional about which habits develop. This is why learning to build healthy routines can have massive impacts on our overall heath: our spirit, our soul, and our body.

VISION

My life has been marked by Proverbs 29:18

"Where there is no vision the people live without restraint..."

That is a wild thought!

In this book of wisdom for living, we are told that if we live without vision the byproduct is an unrestrained life. I know that for some readers this "do whatever I want lifestyle" may sound like an appealing promise. Much of our culture wants us to believe that freedom is when there is no one telling you how to live, what to say, or how to think; the realities of God, however, say the opposite. God says that when we live with restraint (or self-control or boundaries, if that language is easier to digest), we are prepared to experience more love and joy and peace, what Paul called "the fruit of the Spirit."

A life without restraint can take various shapes and forms: staying up later than we should, overconsumption of food or material things, wasting our time in the scroll-hole (Instagram, TikTok, Facebook, YouTube, whatever one you like best), and giving ourselves to things that do not help now or into eternity.

Nehemiah's story in the Bible is a great story of how vision can help us to live for the glory of God and the good of others. After the temple had been destroyed, Nehemiah had a desire to rebuild the temple and he committed himself to doing it, no matter what. God saw the commitment Nehemiah had and blessed it. The vision that Nehemiah had was able to carry him forward until the work was done. Nehemiah had to cut off distractions, believe in his identity when faced with ridicule, and had to show up each day to finish what God had put on his heart to begin. No matter what opposition or obstacles Nehemiah encountered, he continued to show up.

Now, most of us are probably not trying to rebuild the destroyed walls of a city that God has put on our hearts (though maybe some of you are). However, we are all carried by our vision or lack of vision forward in life. I don't believe that we can emphasize enough how important vision is for living our lives:

The greater our vision, the easier our decision making becomes.

The easier our decision making becomes, the easier it is to live in alignment with our calling and identity.

The more we live in alignment with our calling and identity, the more we live with an overflow of love and joy and peace.

One of the beautiful things about getting vision for your season is that it provides us with the power to restrain ourselves from what would distract us. There will always be distractions that come to sabotage our peace and purpose in this life. The good news is that we have the ability to anchor ourselves to peace and purpose by creating healthy rhythms and routines for our lives.

CHART THE COURSE AHEAD

I believe that most people are wanting to live lives that are happy and healthy. For readers who are from or live in the United States, the country was literally founded on the belief that everyone has the right to be happy:

...among these [rights] are life, liberty, and the pursuit of *happiness*.

Modern research has shown that the people who are happiest are those who live in intentional routine. If the research alone isn't convincing enough for you, these findings affirm God's design as told in Scripture. God created the world to have seasons. God created morning & evening. When giving Israel structure for their community, God created the "Year of Jubilee," which happened every fifty years and involved releasing debt, setting all prisoners free, setting all slaves free, returning all property to its original owner, and ceasing from all work for one year (more on this in a minute). All this is to say that God cared deeply about the rhythm of life, specifically around work and rest.

As a father of seven children, I have seen the way a predictable routine benefits children to feel safe and provides a structure for them to grow into their God-given identity. As a mentor to many people over my life, I have seen how routines provide a sense of purpose by removing excess decision fatigue. When our lives lack order or structure, we are like wild vines growing in many directions and unable to bear fruit. Rhythms and routines are the lattice, the support structure, on which we can continue to grow, mature, and in the words of Jesus, "bear much fruit."

Now, as easy as it is for me to talk about the importance and benefits of rhythm and routine in our lives, the reality is that it is much easier said than done. The reality is that there is a very real enemy who wants to sabotage your growth, your identity, and your peace.

I believe that the greatest enemy we face in this age is distraction. This has been talked about at length and there are many great books on the subject, but we have to acknowledge the role of distraction in our lives before we can move on. Think about how easy it is to open up your phone to check one thing, only to end up checking in on a million other things, completely forgetting why you opened your phone in the first place.

Just me?

I have found that I live most in line with my calling and identity not by trying to be undistracted, but by doubling down on the vision that God has given me for my life. Once I have caught the vision, I work with God to create rhythms and routines that can support that calling and identity.

Here's the best part:

The more I live in alignment with my calling & identity, the more I see myself living in love and joy and peace.

Living in alignment is what Jesus talked about when He mentioned the "easy yoke" and the "light burden" that is recorded in Matthew chapter eleven. It is the type of living that Eugene Peterson summarized as living "freely and lightly." I believe that most of, if not all of, the tiredness, the soul-level fatigue, and the burnout we experience stems from living out of alignment with who we are called to be. When we work against design, we make life harder and often feel a lot more tired than we ought to be.

This is why discovering who God is and who you are always pays massive dividends, both today and in the future. The more we see Him and align our life with Him, the more clearly we see who we are and where we are heading in life.

NOTHING NEW UNDER THE SUN

If you study the lives of people you look up to, people who made breakthroughs in their respective lanes, you will be hard-pressed to find people who lived without routine. You will see people who had a vision for what they wanted and created the structure to support their vision. You will see people who understood that achieving what they ultimately wanted required delaying gratification in the moment so that they could receive satisfaction in the future.

In western cultures today, there is an assault on structure. There are many who believe that any external rules or regulations are negative because they inhibit self-expression. The reality, however, is that even un-routine is a form of routine. You either choose the routine and trajectory of your life, or the routine chooses you and the trajectory of your life will follow.

Now, this does not mean rhythms or routines are one-size fits all. There is a joy in the exploration and finding what works for you in any given season. That being said, we are all created in the image of God and there are systems that speak to that identity and help us to experience the free and easy life that we talked about earlier. One of these is the relationship that we have with work and rest, and finding the correct balance with each.

WORK AND REST

Jesus was raised in a culture that believed in God's systems for optimizing the health of people, communities, and ultimately the world. In Genesis, we see that God creates and then there is "evening and morning" each day. This may not seem important to us as modern readers, but God was revealing the importance of beginning our days with rest: this means that we enter into each day with sleep and we end each day with reflection on the faithfulness of God.

I used to say, "win the morning to win the day," but over the last year, I have seen more and more that the evening is the first domino to fall when it comes to winning the day. My new motto is "win the evening to win the morning, and inevitably win the day." It's not as catchy, but it is much more accurate. This mental shift of placing emphasis on winding down and resting well has led me into greater health in many areas. I now see that the golden hour of my day is the last hour before I go to bed, though, I definitely rely on God to help me use it well.

The research coming out these days estimates that over ninety percent of people end their day looking at their phones. On top of this, the same ninety percent are reported to be waking up only to do the same exact thing.

Plug-in to the dopamine machine, shut our eyes, open them, & repeat.

The research is in agreement that this is wreaking havoc on our sleep, emotional health, and ability to live as we desire (if you are curious about any of this, I highly recommend reading some of the research that is coming out of Cleveland Clinic and Harvard). The craziest thing about this is that we are still in the infant stages of researching the effect that these devices are having on our lives. We still have no idea what the compound effect will be of these behaviors over the coming decades.

In Isaiah 50, we read a prophetic poem about Jesus' relationship with the Father where it says, "He awakens me morning by morning, He awakens my ear to listen as a disciple."

Did we catch that?

Jesus had a morning routine: morning after morning being with his Father and posturing His heart to listen to God. I like to say that if Jesus needed it, I probably do too. Any day that we wake up to be with God and commit our day to Him is starting our day with a win. Finding a rhythm that allows us to behold God before beholding anything else sows seeds that will bear much fruit in the course of our lives.

Human beings thrive with a healthy amount of structure. Too much and we try to find an escape like an animal in a cage, too little and we are tugged on a leash by whichever algorithm knows us best.

If you have ever had a small collection of books to display, you know that bookends are an essential.

Without bookends on each side of your collection, it is impossible for the books to stand up straight. Our evening and morning routine are the bookends of our days. After twenty plus years of mentoring countless lives, I would say it is one of the greatest factors for staying healthy and whole over the long-haul.

I have seen many casualties in the war for our hearts. More often than not, what ends up taking people out is misplaced affection. When our affections are in the wrong place, we plateau in Christ, and from there it is only a matter of time before we become unsatisfied and unwilling to carry on. This is why the flashy things don't impress me anymore. I am impressed by committed relationships, what Eugene Peterson called "long obedience in the same direction." That is what I am hoping to leave you with in this chapter: nothing new, just ancient tried-and-true wisdom for the road ahead.

A HARD RESET

I can't end this section without mentioning a program I developed to upgrade the body, soul, and spirit: *The 60 Day Challenge*. This challenge was created in a season when I was diligently seeking the Lord for ways to grow and develop people in Christ. In all honesty, I really believe that God gave me a clear and simple path for how to do this, based simply on the fact that this type of challenge is not something I would create on my own. If you are seeking ways to increase your health in all areas and grow in intimacy with God, I encourage you to check out the website: join60daychallenge.com

I am not looking to exaggerate the impact of this challenge, but in my twenty years of ministry, I have never received so much positive feedback. The most common word used to describe it is "life-changing" (I guess that's two words, haha). People have been healed of skin conditions, stomach problems, anxiety, and experienced greater energy simply from the rhythms presented in this challenge. My favorite testimonies though are the ones when people tell me they have never felt closer to Jesus. There are testimonies sprinkled throughout the book about the impact that it has had on those who finished it. I would also encourage you to count the cost before joining though, because it will call you to level-up your life in many areas, which takes time and commitment to do. The challenge is a hard reset, and it is guaranteed to upgrade your body, soul, and spirit. Lastly, I would encourage you to find a companion or group for the journey. Like life, the challenge can have very difficult moments, and it is always much harder to experience these moments alone.

The 60 Day Challenge is just one flavor of rhythm and routine. Again, the key is finding the rhythms and routines that fit how God has uniquely made you. When we are living in these routines, we are able to live in full alignment with ourselves and God, leading to a more healthy body, soul, and spirit. This allows us to show up each day more present to God and those around us, living from the blessings of rhythm and routines and becoming a blessing to those around us.

CHAPTER 3 REFLECTION QUESTIONS

1. What stood out to you most from this chapter? Why do you think that is? How could you apply this?

2. Do you find that you naturally embrace rhythms and routines, or do you fight against them? Why do you think that is? Invite the Holy Spirit to speak to you about your relationship to structure.

3. What do you find gets most in the way of a healthy rhythm or routine in your life? How could you eliminate that block?

CHAPTER 4: THE STORIES WE TELL

We are all storytellers. Research has shown that we retain information most easily when things are laid out in stories that we can easily follow and understand. Humans have always identified most easily with stories because that is how we experience life; not in data points and facts, but in rising action, climax, and conclusion.

This is why Jesus came to people as a storyteller. He understood that in order to show people what God and Heaven were like, He would need to communicate with stories that were relatable - stories that would help people to imagine a deeper reality than the one they were experiencing.

Now, not all stories are easy to understand. In fact, there are times when the same story is interpreted differently by different hearers, depending on their history and their perspective. Whether it's adults reporting on an important event or siblings recalling a disagreement to their parents, we see that our lens affects the way that we experience the world around us.

During one of Jesus' teachings, which we often refer to as the "Sermon on the Mount," He communicated the importance of understanding, believing, and living life based on His stories. Jesus said that if we build our lives on sand (a false story that results in false living) then, when the storms of life come, our lives will crumble under the shaking; however, if we build our lives on the rock (the story God tells that results in a life of love), then when the storms of life come, we will remain strong and upright. This is the power that stories have: they will determine whether we crumble or stand.

True, not every story that we tell ourselves about a person or a situation will ruin our entire life. However, some stories can drastically impact our experiences. This is especially true when it comes to the stories we tell about who God is, who we are, and what has happened to us.

STORYMAKERS AND STORYTELLERS

Each of us is a storymaker and a storyteller. Inside our heads, we are constantly interpreting the events around us and making meaning of those experiences. The stories we tell ourselves about the world often become the experience we have in the world, and the same is true of our thoughts about God. Consider these questions in relation to your thoughts about God:

Does God deeply love the entire world?

Is God a loving Father who wants to embrace and be with His children regardless of their behavior?

Does my view of God the Father look the same as my view of Jesus?

Do I look forward to spending time with God and getting to know Him more?

There is no amount of words that could fully capture how much God loves each of us. However, this truth is constantly under scrutiny, as is the story we are telling about God. The world that we live in is full of loss, pain, and senseless acts of destruction. This book is not here to address the dilemma of good and evil, but I will say that Jesus understands that tension and demonstrated how to live in it by His act on the cross. Despite betrayal and injustice, Jesus walked in forgiveness and love, modeling what a life surrendered to the character of God looks like.

We live in a fallen world. As much as we may desire it, we simply cannot know everything there is to know about life; however, what we can know is that God is good, loving, and unchanging. We can tell the same story about God that God has forever been telling about Himself: a story of hope in every season and a love that our world so desperately needs.

The stories that I want to tell myself, my kids, and my kid's kids one day is the story that is displayed in scripture: God is with us, for us, and never against us, no matter what experience of life we are having. This story will always be challenged by what is happening around us and lies from the enemy. This is why we need to know the story of God — the story of a God who did not intend for death, disease or destruction to be our reality. Despite this intention, from the garden forward, humanity has made choices that do not always align with the kingdom of God and the realities of heaven. This is why when Jesus modeled prayer to the disciples, He prayed that the Father's kingdom come and will be done, on earth as it is in heaven.

We are now invited by God to be active participants in bringing more of heaven to earth. We are invited to align our lives and prayers with the story that God wants to tell all of humanity — a better story, a redemptive story, a story that can heal our image of Him and love for humanity.

HOW TO TELL A BETTER STORY

If we want to live a healthy life in God, then we can't afford to tell stories about Him that are not true.

Now maybe you're thinking:

What you are saying makes sense. I understand how what I think about God would affect how I interact with God, but I don't understand how to just start thinking differently about God. Am I just supposed to change my mind?

In scripture, there are two primary ways that we can change our understanding of what God is like: the renewing of our mind[1] and beholding God.[2] It is wonderful news that we are promised by the grace of God, and the work of the Holy Spirit, that when we align with God's ways, transformation is going to happen. However, if we want to experience that transformation, we need to ask ourselves a very important question:

Are we beholding the God revealed to us by Jesus and renewing our minds with His word?

Another way to think about this is with the following question:

If others could read our minds, what would they learn about who God is? Are the thoughts that we are meditating on about God the Father inline with the same Father that Jesus came to reveal?

Our view of God should make it easy to connect with Him and make us feel safe to talk with Him about all areas of our life. If we are hiding from God or afraid to open our lives up to Him, then we may want to reconsider the theology that we have about Him. The way that we think of God will ultimately determine our health in life: physical, mental, and spiritual.

STORIES WE TELL ABOUT GOD

In his book '*The Knowledge of the Holy,*' A.W. Tozer penned this famous line:

"What we think about God is the most important thing about us."[3]

I want you to read that quote again slowly.

"What we think about God is the most important thing about us."

Based on my experience, I can think of very few statements I agree with as much as I do that one. Our understanding of who God is and what God is like will shape every single thing about who we are. When it is all said and done, we will end up becoming like whatever we give our attention to. In other words, we become what we behold. This is great news if you believe that God is a God of love, joy, and peace. However, it is a much different story if your God is angry, judgmental, and impatient.

When we know that someone is glad to be with us, we find it a joy to see them and spend time with them. When we know that someone has disdain, disgust, or anger towards us, we find it's easier to shut down and avoid being around that person. Children are wired to come alive when they see that their parent's eyes are filled with gladness and love for them. They will want to spend time with that parent. However, if a child walks into a room and sees their parent angry or in distress, they will naturally avoid interacting with that parent.

This is why we must be very careful about what we allow to shape our view and understanding of God.

Jesus made many bold statements during His life, and one of the boldest was this:

"If you have seen me, then you have seen the Father."

At some level, the entire world struggles with the Father-God distortion. Most people view God the Father in a negative and unfavorable light. Even those of us who have a decent view of God as a Father can still have a bit of suspicion about the goodness of God and the ways that it manifests in our lives. This is part of why Jesus had to come to earth: to bring clarity to our distorted image of God as a Father.

When Jesus said, "If you have seen me, then you have seen the Father," He told the world exactly what God is like. This means that the face of God the Father looks exactly like the face of Jesus. This means that the character of Jesus is the character of God the Father. This means that the love Jesus showed the world is the same love that God the Father showed the world. There is no other God than the God that Jesus came to reveal to this world. No God hiding behind Jesus, no God different than Jesus. Chapter one of the book of Hebrews speaks a similar message, saying that Jesus is the "exact representation of the Father's nature."

In my opinion, what we think about God as Father will impact our lives more than any other belief we have. If God is not loving, understanding, patient, and good, then we will inevitably live our lives at some level avoiding God. To live every day with a God who is against you or withholds love from you based on behavior will make it impossible to enjoy your life. Telling yourself the true story of a God who finds you valuable enough to die for is the path towards a healthy and joyful life.

STORIES WE TELL ABOUT OURSELVES

The stories that we tell about ourselves — about who we were, who we are, and who we are becoming — are often impacted by forces outside

of ourselves. Usually, these stories come from things that happened to us or were said about us when we were younger. The key to living a truer story, and experiencing deeper healing in life, is always found when we align our thoughts with God's thoughts about ourselves.

None of us are born into this world with a healthy thought life. Healthy thought lives must be cultivated like a garden, allowing the grace of God to water the good thoughts and help uproot the unhealthy thoughts. Some of us were raised in healthier environments than others, and this is a blessing that leads to less unlearning; however, nobody makes it through childhood without mixed messages or without picking up some stinkin' thinkin' along the way.

Have you ever considered where the thoughts that fill your mind each day come from?

The mind is always working, for some of us a little too much. Our minds are powerful, for better and for worse. For those of us who have a healthy thought life, we will have a perspective that is mostly saturated with satisfaction and joy, regardless of circumstances. However, for those of

us with an unhealthy thought life, our perspective is usually distorted and we become saturated with fear and worry. No matter how you spin it, the thoughts that we cultivate will determine how we experience our life. Another way to say that is our feelings are the byproduct of our thoughts.

TRAUMA CAN WRITE AN UNTRUE STORY

Many of us will experience things that are very difficult in this life. When these difficult or traumatic events happen, we often unconsciously create stories about ourselves that affect how we interpret and interact with the world around us. Oftentimes, when we go through these traumatic events, we unconsciously create stories about our identity based on the event.

Now, I am not saying that the stories we tell ourselves are always untrue, but if we are not aware of the stories that we create about ourselves from challenging experiences, they can often dominate our outlook on life. As someone who has walked with countless people through painful moments, I am not at all belittling what people have gone through, so please do not think that. Trauma and pain need to be heard, felt, validated,

Now if we want to not only get free, but stay free, we may have to walk down a path that we normally may not be accustomed to walking. It is a path that only knows unconditional love, forgiveness, and grace for all people at all times. Forgiveness is the oxygen of the kingdom of God. We cannot be free while holding other people hostage in our hearts. The key to walking in forgiveness is knowing that God will be with you on the path and is committed to showing you the way through. According to Scripture, this path only gets brighter and brighter each day. God made us to heal and walk in greater wholeness as we go through life. We can only do this if we allow God to set us truly free, and true freedom involves freeing others as well.

THE TRUTH OF TRANSFORMATION

I hesitate to share what has been helpful in my process of knowing God because I am aware that each journey is unique. Despite the hesitation, I also feel compelled to share a few things because I have seen them produce what Jesus called "fruit that remains." What I mean is that there are helpful ways of living that have led to more love, more joy, and more peace in my life, which are the byproducts of time spent beholding God.

One thing that has deeply connected me with the heart of the Father is music. I love the Word of God, and I don't know of a better way to get my mind renewed than filling it with God's thoughts about who He is and who I am. However, listening to truth through music has had a similar impact on my life too. There are many artists who have helped me to see the Father in a new way because of how they spoke about Him. Jason Upton, as well as Jonathan and Melissa Helser, are two examples that have left lasting impacts on my life. I will be eternally grateful for the lyrics in various songs that God has used to renew my mind and open my heart more to His experiential love.

Music has a special way of connecting the head and the heart. This is why listening to music that speaks about God's character and thoughts is so important: God has a way of taking truth from a song and driving out lies that have shackled us for years. We live in a generation that is quick to move from one thing to the next, but I am not exaggerating when I say that there are some songs that I have listened to hundreds of times because they continued to illuminate different aspects of who God is and who I am to Him. The mind is a beautiful thing, and knowing about God is valuable for our relationship with God, but deep transformation will always take place in the heart.

Read these lyrics to "I Lose My Ability" by Jonathan and Melissa Helser slowly (then afterward listen to the song a few times):

"I lose my ability to be afraid
When I hear You say my name
All the voices that once filled my head
They are gone when you speak
When I see Your face
Everything changes
In the radiance of Your smile
You got this way of
Chasing away those
Shadows that hang around"

THE WORD TELLS A BETTER STORY

Now, another rhythm of life that has been beyond helpful is having a relationship with God through the Word of God. While I love music and have found it incredibly helpful for changing how I think about and experience God, the Word of God has been the greatest gift for me when it comes to cultivating intimacy and understanding.

When it comes to reading the Word, we are joining right thinking with heartfelt connection. We are not reading the Word for more knowledge, but to know God as a husband would know his wife. For example, if a plumber came to my house when I was not home and accomplished what needed to be done, I would be thankful. However, if my neighbor asked me about his character, what he is like, stories about his family, etc., I would be clueless how to answer. To know God relationally means knowing more than just the work He has accomplished; it means to know Him from the heart — from the place of connection, oneness, and intimacy. Real change from the inside out comes from hearing God in relationship. This means that when we approach the Bible, we need to do so with an understanding that God is kind and loving and wants to spend time with us. We come with an expectation of hearing God and responding back to Him in the place of prayer. This is how we grow relationship and a familiar friendship with God over time.

I want to give you three verses to meditate on. I highly encourage you to write them down on 3x5 cards, put them to memory, and most importantly, talk to God about them. Each of these verses has had a profound impact on my relationship with God, my view of myself, and the lens that I view life through. It is hard to exaggerate the impact that each of these verses has had on my life. I have built history with God and a deeper life in Him from meditating on these verses:

COLOSSIANS 2:8-9

"See to it that no one takes you captive through hollow and deceptive philosophy, which depends on human tradition and the elemental spiritual forces of this world rather than on Christ. For in Christ all the fullness of deity lives in bodily form and *in Him you have been made complete.*"

The current church culture in most places is an arrival culture: a culture where we are focused far more on outcomes than on process. This means that we are always trying to end up somewhere or be seen as a certain type of person in order to feel satisfied. The culture of the kingdom, however, is a discovery culture. In a discovery culture, we aren't trying to obtain something, rather we are trying to discover what God has already given to us. This is what verse nine is telling us about in the passage above. If you would like, please read that last verse again:

"For in Christ all the fullness of deity lives in bodily form and *in Him you have been made complete.*"

Crazy, right!?

According to God, we aren't broken, we don't have something wrong with us, and we don't need fixing. According to God, we simply need to discover that we are whole in Christ. We have been made complete in Christ. This truth has massive implications because it takes away all striving to become something or someone and helps us to rest in the beautiful truth that we are made whole.

I love how Song of Songs 4:7 describes this truth. Speaking about the way that God sees us, the author writes, "You are altogether beautiful, my darling, and there is no blemish in you." The more that this reality — the reality that God sees you and loves everything about you — sinks in, the more whole you will become.

The journey of discovering is an adventure in which God convinces us more and more that He did not make a mistake when He created us. We are a masterpiece, He has good thoughts about us at all times, and His arms are always wide-open no matter what we have done. This way of relating to and doing life with God is very different from trying to earn God's affection.

When God raised us to new life with Christ, He didn't remodel our old three bedroom home. It wasn't enough for God to give us a new coat of interior paint and call it a day. Instead, God tore down the old house and in its place gave us our dream home. This new home doesn't need fixing or repairs, it is perfect.

I know that this idea can ruffle some feathers, but this is a key to unlocking freedom and wholeness in your life. Once you align your thoughts with God's, the natural way of life becomes supernatural. We wake up differently and live from an entirely different starting point than we did before. Again, we are not trying to arrive, but rather we are discovering who we already are in God. We are trusting the Holy Spirit each day to grow our belief in what God has already said is true about us.

2 PETER 1:4

"Through these He has given us His very great and precious promises, so that through them *you may participate in the divine nature*, having escaped the corruption in the world caused by evil desires."

This verse is important because it redefines our identity, telling us that we are participants in the divine nature. Please don't miss this:

You have one nature as a believer, and that is the divine nature.

Not a sin nature.

You are a participant in the divine nature.

This means that because of what Jesus has done, you have the very nature of God. This means you are much more similar to God than you may be aware of. The book of Corinthians puts it a little differently, saying that you have been given "the mind of Christ," meaning access to think and live like God.

As an image bearer, we have our father's DNA:

Daddy's Natural Attributes.

This truth is radical and transformational, allowing us to rest in God. This truth allows us to let go of the need to perfect ourselves and instead allows Jesus to live His life through us. There is a reason that when the angel announced the coming of Jesus, they said it was good news of great joy for all people. As we let truth, good news, and a better narrative shape us, we begin to experience life that we never knew was possible. We are able to live a life caught up in experiencing God's heart and learning how He designed us to live, a life made in His exact image and growing more each day into His likeness.

ROMANS 8:31-39

"What, then, shall we say in response to these things? If God is for us, who can be against us? He who did not spare His own Son, but gave Him up for us all — how will He not also, along with Him, graciously give us all things? Who will bring any charge against those whom God has chosen? It is God who justifies. Who then is the one who condemns? No one. Christ Jesus who died — more than that, who was raised to life — is at the right hand of God and is also interceding for us. Who shall separate us from the love of Christ? Shall trouble or hardship or persecution or famine or nakedness or danger or sword? As it is written:

For your sake we face death all day long; we are considered as sheep to be slaughtered.

No, in all these things we are more than conquerors through Him who loved us. For I am convinced that neither death nor life, neither angels nor demons, neither the present nor the future, nor any powers, neither height nor depth, nor anything else in all creation, will be able to separate us from the love of God that is in Christ Jesus our Lord."

These verses more than any other have shaped the person that I am today. I had a season over a decade ago where I read and re-read these verses over and over and over. It was like God was inviting me to pitch a tent because He knew we would be camping out here for a long time. I would read other things, but every time I would go back to these verses, it felt like heaven was breathing on them afresh. I felt the presence of God doing something in my heart that would change my course of life. It was the kindness of God to do this for me, as I didn't know it at the time, but I would need these verses for things I would face later in life — years that were full of pain, doubt, discouragement, and confusion, years that burned away all the brush and allowed these verses to be the path through the wilderness in my life. These verses became like a set of glasses that gave me twenty-twenty vision when looking at my experiences and different situations that I was facing in life, marriage, parenting, and pastoring.

I still go back to these verses on a monthly basis, allowing myself to be reminded over and over of God's heart and His ways of handling situations in life, both for me and for His people that I get to pastor.

I will often prayerfully say:

"No matter what I do or what has been done to me, I will never be separated from the love of God. God is always for me and never against me. Nothing will ever be big enough to get in the way of God's love in my life.
No mistake.
No shortcoming.

Absolutely nothing."

Sometimes, I insert a name and use this to pray for others rather than myself. When I do this, it helps connect my heart with God's heart for this person. I have always found scriptural prayer to be very powerful in releasing faith and right perspective in life.

In closing, we are all storytellers and storymakers, including God. The good news is that God is committed to writing a better story in all our lives. Or maybe it would be better said, He is rewriting all of our stories to see it through His lens, to see Him for who He really is and see ourselves from our Father's eyes. Regardless of what has happened to us, where we have been, or what we have done, good or bad in this life, when our story becomes His story, we have a true God story. Our history is really His-Story.

CHAPTER 4 REFLECTION QUESTIONS

1. What stood out to you most from this chapter? Why do you think that is? How could you apply this?

2. What stories do you currently tell yourself about God? What is He like? How does he feel about you? Do these stories align with the God revealed in Scripture?

3. What stories do you currently tell yourself that may need to be re-written by God? Invite Holy Spirit to highlight memories to you and then to show you what God thinks about them.

CHAPTER 5: SEASONS OF LIFE

I grew up in Southern California. This means that for most of the year it was seventy-five and sunny, which is great for enjoying the world that God made, but didn't leave me with a proper understanding of the seasons. In order to tell that the seasons were changing, I had to get really good at noticing the small changes that indicated a new season. While this is true of the physical seasons each year, I see a lot of similarities for noticing our spiritual season.

Paul put it this way in 1 Corinthians 15:46:

"The spiritual did not come first, but the natural, and after that the spiritual."

The more aware we are of the season that we are currently in, as well as the season that we are moving towards, the easier it is to stay content with what God has put before us. Life is always changing, and I have noticed it is much more fruitful to learn to move *with* the seasons of life than to move against them. To live a resilient life, a life where we keep our eyes fixed on Jesus, we must learn to keep the seasons in mind.

1 Chronicles 12:32 says that the sons of Issachar understood the times, and as a result, knew what would be best for the entire nation of Israel. These men had the ability to read the spiritual seasons of their nation and respond in wisdom. We must remember that our lives have a much larger impact than simply our own experience. Learning to keep our season in mind will not only lead to greater health and joy in our own lives, but also in the lives of the people around us.

THE CYCLE

Think of the cycle as a circle that continually spins over and over throughout your life. Unlike in the natural, where seasons have short and predictable increments each year, the spiritual seasons can very in length and intensity. However, each relationship, assignment, vocation, or calling will go through these seasons many times throughout one's life.

Each season has a theme attached to it:

Spring — Get Ready

Summer — Let's Do This!

Fall — Doldrums (Boredom, Restlessness, & Loss)

Winter — Cocoon

We will talk about each season in depth, but before getting into the nitty-gritty, I want to start with another Holy Ghost hack that helps to avoid self-sabotage, and transition from season to season well. This hack may sound confusing at first, but as you read through the chapter, I know that it will become more clear.

The hack is this:

Fall is coming, so look to put yourself in winter.

We will talk more about this as we go through the chapter, but for now just remember that the fastest way out of fall is an early winter. This means that because we know that fall is coming, we can dive into our cocoon early and shortchange fall. We will talk more about how to dive into winter, how to utilize the cocoon, and how to keep fall from taking you out as we work through the chapter, but for now let's unpack the seasons.

SPRING: GET READY

Spring is the time where we are anticipating "the new." We are excited for what is on the horizon: new futures, new possibilities, and the new things that God is doing in our lives. We can see the blessings on the horizon. We feel like we can taste the sweetness of what God is going to do, but we have not yet stepped into it.

God designed us for adventure. On the journey of life, we will need to travel new paths, jump off of cliffs, and take risks as we continue the journey into the unknown. Spring is the time when we are getting ready to take one of these risks, when God is preparing us for something that He wants to do in our lives.

During this time, we feel a general understanding of where God is taking us, we just aren't completely in it yet. In order to do spring well, we need to cultivate a practice of asking the Holy Spirit how to use the time most effectively so that we can begin summer with a "let's do this" attitude.

SUMMER: LET'S DO THIS

Summer is the time when we get to play. We are beginning the work that God prepared for us and we have a lot of momentum behind us. This is the season that people enjoy the most, and thus, have the hardest time leaving it behind. Hence, we get the term "endless summer."

Summer is the time of excitement. It is moving to a new place and exploring. It is starting a new role and dreaming about all the things you are going to learn and do. It is starting a new relationship and experiencing the butterflies and joys of young love. It may even be experiencing a perspective shift and viewing life through a new lens. Summer is the time when things are new, enjoyment is easy, and gratitude flows naturally from what we do. Summer feels really good, which is what is dangerous about it.

Like I said, many people have a hard time leaving summer. We know the seasons must change, but we often resist it with all our might. Even though the things that once served us aren't working anymore, we spend time and energy trying to make them work for us. When we live with an "endless summer" mentality, we end up frustrated. In the endless summer, we begin to question where God went and why things that once felt effortless are beginning to feel like work.

Not all humans, but many humans, resist change. We like ritual and habit, and we will try to hold onto something even if we know it is not serving us the way it once was. This is what happens in the endless summer; we are longing for the past when things were easier instead of living in the present and asking what God wants to do now. This is when we begin the transition from summer into fall.

FALL: DOLDRUMS

The doldrums are inevitable in life. This is the time where we often feel bored, restless, and a sense of loss. Fall is the season where it feels like something is dying: an ideal, a way of doing things, a mindset, a commitment, etc. Despite these intense feelings, fall is not something that is inherently negative. Oftentimes, a sense of loss in one area of life indicates the life to come in a different area. Fall is a necessary part of continuing to live an empowered, healthy, and joyful life in God.

When we move to a new place, begin a new relationship, or start a new job, we should enjoy the new and exciting; however, we must also understand that the doldrums are coming. Oftentimes, we are not prepared for the seasons of boredom and loss, which lead us to believe that something is wrong rather than notice we are moving into a new season. As a result, fall tends to take many people out because they look outward for things to bring them comfort rather than looking inward to the Comforter.

The doldrums have little to no excitement about them, hence the reason most people quickly become restless, bored, and frustrated. When these uncomfortable emotions arise, it is common to start "rearranging furniture." We often think the issue is "out there" and that if we can just change ___________, then we will be happy. Think about it, how many times has this thought crossed your mind:

If only I was doing that job, then I would finally be happy.

If only I was living in that place, then I would be living my best life.

If I was in that relationship, then things would be easy.

The problem with these thoughts is they are simply excuses for not doing the internal work to develop a healthy, empowered, and joyful you.

The doldrums will often ask us to let go of something in order to have open hands for what God is wanting to give us next. Learning to embrace the open-handed approach to life is a key ingredient in doing this fall season well. When we are young, this has fewer consequences because our primary impact is on ourself. As we grow older, however, the impact of this discontentment not only lands on us, but our friends, families, and communities. I want to say this again:

Fall is not a negative thing; it is necessary for our growth in God.

Selah.

In spring and summer, we are focused and energized by what we are doing or anticipating, making it much easier to avoid distraction. In fall, as our excitement begins to decrease, it becomes much easier to seek relief outside of God. This means that fall is also the season where sin is more appealing than ever.

King David's life is a classic example of how fall can take us out. 2 Samuel 11 begins with this phrase: "In the spring, when kings go off to war…" For those of you who are not familiar with King David's story, David was a warrior at heart. It was his vocation, his calling. At the time when the king should have been at war, David ended up staying behind, and in his restlessness, slept with another man's wife. David should have been at war, but he forgot his assignment and his identity. This is often the case when we despise the fall and don't understand the necessity of putting ourselves into winter.

Fall can feel inactive, stagnate, and boring. These feelings of restlessness are very normal. These feelings are not meant to be numbed out, but to be embraced. We need to use them as a springboard into conversational intimacy with God. These moments can create questions about how we are doing and what we are doing with our lives, which are perfect questions to discuss with the God who made us. This is a very normal part of life and if we allow it, it is the place where God does a deeper work in us.

WINTER - COCOON

Now back to the hack: fall is coming, so look to put yourself in winter. The secret to avoid being taken out or self-sabotaging during the fall (doldrums) is to use the fall as the sign to enter winter. The fall season was designed to deepen our lives and signal us to enter the winter. Winter is when we enter the cocoon and we can reignite our vision, remember our design, and recall who we really are.

Winter is the time when we allow God to do something new in our lives, and remind us of what He has already said. Remember this is a Holy Ghost hack, which should make more sense now that we understand the other seasons. We must learn to dive into the cocoon early so that we can avoid self-sabotaging in the fall. The cocoon is the place where we are able to protect ourselves from doing something we would regret later, and instead reflect on what the Father is wanting to reveal to us.

The cocoon is where we remind ourselves of our "why" for our lives. The cocoon is essentially making space and time to remind ourselves of the truth said about us and grow our conversational connection with God. It is a time to talk to God about our unique wiring, prophetic words, purpose etc., and learn to double-down on your strengths instead of fixating on weaknesses. This is why we must learn to develop a cocoon mentality: a lifestyle and rhythm of reflection. A cocoon mentality allows us to be aware of who God is and what God is doing in our lives.

In winter, we must allow ourselves to lock eyes with our Father and hear the words that He is speaking about our lives. When we start to feel the stagnation and boredom of the fall, it is a sign to increase the amount of conversation we have with God about our lives. Instead of self-sabotaging by moving too fast, or falling into boredom and complacency, we must begin to move slow and seek God's perspective so that we can rest in the discomfort of our current season.

GETTING REAL

I have been very blessed to be married to a remarkable woman for over twenty years. I have been involved in the church that I helped to start for over twenty years. I have lived in the same city for over twenty years. While doing all of these things, I have worked two part-time jobs alongside my duties as a full-time pastor. These are the callings and commitments that are on my life and in all transparency, I have wanted to quit or pivot multiple times from all of them. I have gone through the fall multiple times in these areas and each time (due to the cocoon of winter), it has birthed something more beautiful and sustainable. That is where one of my life mantras comes from:

If you don't quit, you win.

It would have been easy to give up or change it up, but I knew that God was asking me to stay where He planted me. God has used fall to help me see Him more clearly, removing the things that are less important to help me focus on what is most important. Cultivating a cocoon mentality — consistently reflecting on what God is saying and doing — is what has helped to sustain me in these seasons. I cringe to think of where my life would be without His voice to remind, settle, and bring clarity to my many fall seasons.

As first generation Christians, my wife and I have walked through many challenges together: pioneering a church, raising seven kids, homeschooling those kids, experiencing multiple miscarriages, and living in a revolving-door, ever-changing college town. We have had to do a lot of unlearning and relearning, but I have noticed that when we move with the seasons God is bringing us through, we have a much healthier perspective.

The more I cultivate a cocoon mentality, the more I see fall as the birthplace of greater strength and vision. Using the secret place to be, think, journal, pray, cry, dream, and read God's word has been irreplaceable in strengthening my understanding of who He is and what He is like.

I have a note in my phone titled "Life Vision" that I revisit almost weekly. This note has my mission in life, five descriptions of who I am, notes on my identity, personality types, prophetic words, and more. I even keep my life verses in here so that I can meditate on them monthly. This all helps me to endure, continue hoping, and keep my eyes on what is important. All of this reminds me of who God is and what He has made me for. This life vision note is a call back to God, and has become a place for connection, conversation, and communion between God and me. Learning to ask questions about who I am, what God loves about me, and allowing myself to receive insight has been vital to the life I live in Him and for Him.

FINAL THOUGHTS

Nowadays, it is not very common to meet someone with a cocoon mentality. Most people are moving too fast to take the time to be with God, connect to His heart, and listen to His voice. However, the age old saying is still true: you make time for what is important to you. I'm going to say that again and invite you to reflect on what your time says about your values:

You make time for what is important to you.

When we allow the Holy Spirit to teach us to slow down for union with God, we are on the path to a healthy and joyful life in God. We need to give God the space to remind us why we decided to follow Him. We need to give God the space to remind us how we are designed. Most importantly, we need to give God the space to remind us who we belong to.

To develop a cocoon mentality, we need to cultivate a rhythm of being with God. We must make time to connect, reflect, and process, regardless of what season we are in. The more that we make time to talk to God about our lives, the more clear our vision and our "why" become, and the more purpose we are able to live with. Slowing down to live at God's pace is the secret to living in your identity and experiencing the life that God has in store for us.

Remember: slow is fast.

Don't become discouraged if it takes time to develop a cocoon mentality. Most of us have trained ourselves to go to God when life is hard, but cruise when things are easy. We have to re-program ourselves to cultivate a cocoon mentality year round, to know that fall is coming, and to see it as an invitation to put ourselves into winter.

This is a process that God wants to engage in with you, not a mindset God wants you to arrive at. There are many starting places: a morning walk, a sabbath retreat, five minutes in your car to check-in with God before you walk into your house, etc. Whatever you can give is meaningful to God; the important part is that you don't give up. God designed us to go through seasons in our marriage, relationships, vocation, and rhythms in life. May we not despise the wisdom of God, but instead learn to embrace the cycles of life. He is a good Father, who is present in every season we experience in life.

CHAPTER 5 REFLECTION QUESTIONS

1. What stood out to you most from this chapter? Why do you think that is? How could you apply this?

2. Have you gone through the doldrums before? If so, how did you get through it? If not, how could you begin cultivating a cocoon mentality for when you do?

3. Which of the four seasons do you most identify with? What do you feel like God is inviting you to learn in this season?

CHAPTER 6: THERE IS ALWAYS A SOLUTION

About five years ago, my wife and I drove to a marriage seminar that was roughly ten hours away from where we lived. We thought of it as a time to clean out some of the leftover residue from the messes we had walked through over fifteen years of birthing and raising children, birthing and raising a church, and just being humans married to another human. We had everything in order and were looking forward to the seminar; the only tricky part was that we had a one-year-old with us who required constant supervision. The seminar days were very full: Monday through Friday from about nine in the morning to six in the evening. You could say it was more of a marriage bootcamp than a marriage seminar.

The day before the seminar was to begin, while we were on our drive, we received a call from the person who was going to watch our baby, saying that they were no longer available. I'm sure you can imagine the panic that my wife and I experienced as we realized that we had no backup plan for this situation. We knew a few people who lived in the town we were going to, so we began making calls, seeing if we could find a solution to our newly discovered problem. We began calling friends, friends of friends, and friends of friends of friends, until eventually we connected with a dad in the area who was willing to help us out. While we were on the phone with this man, he said something that profoundly impacted my life from that moment forward:

There is *always* a solution.

On the surface, this simple statement may not seem like a deep revelation into the heart of God or ourselves, but in the midst of everything we were feeling, these words instantly drained the worry and anxiety that was filling up our hearts.

There is always a solution.

This word was spoken from the Father through a father straight into my heart. God was reminding me that there is no problem I will encounter that cannot be solved with and through my partnership with Him. This statement was an invitation to be free from all the worry and concern that I experience when facing obstacles, and the many problems that come up in life. What God revealed to me was a profound truth that can only be experienced from adopting a new mindset:

God goes before me, and has already made provision for me in every situation in my life.

There is always a solution.

Looking back, it was from this moment forward that I viewed life through a different lens. Prior to this, I knew God loved me, but something was out of order. Like a spiritual chiropractor, God used this statement to bring my spirit and mind into alignment. Over time, this mindset shift broke off the different layers of orphan thinking that I had regarding obstacles, and it allowed me to enter deeper into sonship. This was my invitation to know, deep in my soul, that my Father was working out everything for my good, providing solutions to my problems, and inviting me to trust Him in this process.

I would not describe myself as a worried or anxious person when it comes to the "what ifs" of life; however, I have found that I am not a big fan of unexpected change, interruptions to my plans, or the unpredictability that comes with them. However, the issue with this way of thinking is that most of our lives are going to be filled with unexpected change, interruptions, and will rarely go as planned. I would even go so far to say that problems are numerous and normal as we turn to face life rather than hide from it. Learning to face life and the myriad of problems that come with it, instead of hiding from it, is one way we step into the "more of God" in our lives. Sometimes, problems can even be a clear indicator that we are moving in the right direction.

In Acts 14:22, we are told "through many tribulations we must enter the kingdom of God." Some versions of this verse use the word "hardships," meaning that it is through difficult and problematic events that we enter into a more robust and fruitful life in God. This is why we must allow God to give us a healthy view of problems, obstacles, and trials in order to experience overall health in God.

HOW WE SEE OUR PROBLEMS

Here is some food for thought:

What if our external circumstances are not the real problem?

What if the real problem has more to do with the way that we view the external circumstances?

This is why I am convinced that our outlook oftentimes has greater implications on our well-being than our actual circumstances. Whether we are facing something small or something large, we need to ask ourselves if our perception is in alignment with how God sees the situation. Do we naturally lean toward doubt, discouragement, and disappointment? Or do we naturally lean toward the belief that God is working whatever we are going through for our good and providing for all our needs?

For years, I dealt with doubt, discouragement, and disappointment. I have come to refer to these as "the deadly D's," because they have the potential to take us out in life. From 2007 to 2013, I was both hunted and haunted by these enemies on a weekly basis. I experienced them in my marriage, my finances, the people in my church, and ultimately, they became the lens that I saw life through. The struggles I was facing at this time were very real; however, I see now that much of my struggle was self-inflicted due to the way that I framed the obstacles I was facing at the time.

Today, I find that I am dealing with even more obstacles, trials, and problems on a daily basis. What is different between then and now, is the person I have become. The life that I have in God has created a different perspective and outlook when I face these challenges. What I know now, that I didn't know then, is that my outlook has the power to shift my experience. Rather than viewing my experiences as inhibitors to my dreams and desires, I view them as invitations into deeper trust and intimacy with God.

Though hard to admit, it is impossible to thoroughly enjoy our lives or experience growth without learning to embrace the obstacles. Obstacles are no respecter of people; we will all face them. But what sets some people apart from others is their ability to respond to the obstacles with peace and steadfastness. However, most of us don't feel peace when we come face to face with a challenge. There are three primary ways I have seen people respond to unexpected obstacles in their life:

1. Fear & Frustration
2. Defeat & Helplessness
3. Overwhelm & Anxiety

Now, a brief word on each.

Fear & Frustration: This response means that when things start to go "wrong," you begin to feel afraid of what is coming, which leads to frustration that life is not going as planned. Oftentimes, this comes from placing a magnifying glass over the things that are not working, rather than the things that are going well in your life. This leads us to believe the stories we are telling ourselves about all the ways that life is going wrong, and we end up in a fear cycle. Remember, the stories we tell ourselves is always the story we live out. Fear is a real emotion, but it is also the only emotion that we are reminded by God to challenge: God says to "fear not" about 365 times throughout the Bible — one "fear not" for every day of the year! The good news is that our God is committed to driving out fear from all our lives with His love. [1]

Defeat & Helplessness: This mindset begins with feeling defeated, which results in a loss of hope. Sometimes when we experience an obstacle, we begin to believe that all of life will become an obstacle. If we are not careful, this mindset can lead to self-pity, which is an open door for the enemy in our lives. A mentor of mine once called self-pity "the revolving door for thc demonic." While that language is strong, I think it is important to consider whose thoughts we are listening to in our lives: are we listening to God's voice and what He says about us, or are we listening to lies from some other source? God is always in our corner, leading us from one good thing to another. So if the thoughts you are having are not reminding you of the future glory that awaits you, it is important to consider where they're coming from. God wants each of us to carry the eyes and ears of the virtuous woman in Proverbs 31 who smilies and laughs when she looks into the future.[2]

Overwhelm & Anxiety: This mindset begins with a feeling of overwhelm that leads to full-blown anxiety in our lives. When we view all obstacles as negative, as inhibitors to the "good life," it is very easy to feel overwhelmed by each challenge that comes our way. While this is an easy mindset to slip into, we must remember that we are created for peace. God does not have any desire to crush us beneath the weight of a challenge or obstacle. When we begin to feel anxiety coming on, it can be a good time to ask God what He has in store for us and what He is teaching us through our current circumstances.

Now this is the crazy part:

Not only do these mindsets create problems on an emotional level or in our souls, but they also wreak havoc on our bodies.

The medical community has attested that approximately 90% of all health related issues, both mental and physical, are related to stress. When we live in a perpetual state of frustration, helplessness, and anxiety, it is literally killing us. I believe that part of the reason for this is that God didn't design this to be our normal. What I mean by this is that we were created by God from a place of love and joy and peace, so naturally, when we live outside of these emotional states, it goes against what we were made from and what we were made for. This raises an important question: how do we live close to the heart of God even as we face obstacles and challenges in life? That is what we will talk about in the next section.

HOW WE SEE LIFE

If we want to experience love, joy, and peace in the midst of challenges, we must learn to see them from God's perspective. In order to see things the way God does, we need a new lens to view life from. In my experience, there are three lenses that can invite us into a new way of seeing our circumstances:

1. We trust
2. We learn
3. We give thanks

TRUST

First, we trust.

Oftentimes, obstacles can be gentle reminders to put our trust in God, regardless of what we are facing or feeling. Anytime we put our trust in something outside of God, it is a false security. False securities will always produce insecurities. Read that again:

False securities will always produce insecurities.

Over years of putting my trust in God amidst obstacles I have found that I have deeper security and a strengthened relational root system in God. Trust isn't some formula we enter into, rather it's a lifting of our thoughts and heart to God through whatever we are facing. Most of us would never choose the hard things we have had to walk through in life; but I am convinced these obstacles help us to build history with God and allow God to heal the root causes of many of our problems: our view of God & ourselves. Often the problems we face are magnified by an incorrect view of who God is and what God is like. When I see who God wants to be for me in the midst of my problems, I naturally grow to trust that He is brining solutions to the problems I am facing.

In 2018, our church community needed to raise a ridiculous amount of money to begin laying the foundations for a future missions base. The best part: we only had thirty days to get the money. We had been praying and waiting for two years for the permission to buy the land (the property was on the market the entire time), and when God finally gave us the permission to pursue it, the church had no money, my family had no money, and we had nobody to call who had money! I like to say that we were perfectly set up for a miracle.

I spent each day for those thirty days wearing a wristband that simply stated "God's got this." I prayerfully declared this truth over our situation and thanked God for the money that had come in and would continue to come in. I knew that I could not walk through this obstacle without God shifting my focus from the problem at hand to the person at work: Himself. It doesn't matter what the challenge in the way is, it is always a chance to deepen our trust in God and to learn to believe in His ways more than our own good ideas.

Lastly, it isn't only in overcoming an obstacle that we are able to deepen trust. Sometimes God doesn't solve problems the way that we want. In these moments, it is important that we remember that we serve a God who is good, who works all things for our good, and is much wiser than we could comprehend.

I have experienced so much loss and so many setbacks over the years. However, by the grace of God, I am able to look back and say "thank you" for each thing I have faced. The low parts of my life have expanded my vision for the kingdom of God and living with the end in mind. The obstacles have helped me to not take life personally, and have helped me to lay roots that are deep in God. It is in the disappointments and the pain that we can look at Jesus, a man familiar with suffering, and know that we are in good company.[3] That is why we must trust, then next we need to learn.

LEARN

Obstacles have the power to make you or break you, to grow you or potentially destroy you. If you don't believe that life is happening *for* you, not *to* you, then it will always be a struggle to embrace the challenges of life.

When I reflect on the loss, setbacks, suffering, and pain of my life, I am able to see how they have shaped me for the better. Each and every challenge has taught me invaluable lessons that have upgraded my perspective. I am not saying that I want to relive them, but what I am saying is that I would not be who I am today without them in my life.

One sign of genuine healing is when we are able to look back on our lives with thankfulness. Not necessarily thankful for what went wrong or the loss we experienced, but how we found God is a greater way and watched Him work it all for good.

Now, I am not taking this time to debate why bad things happen in the world or who allows them. I will say with certainty that I don't believe that everything that happens in the world is God's will. I don't believe that Jesus would invite us to pray for heaven to come to earth or for God's will to be done if God's will was in fact already being done.

For me, one thing that has produced some really good fruit in my journey is understanding the exchange rate in the kingdom of God. This exchange rate is simple: my stuff for His stuff. This means that when I give God hardship and pain, I get goodness in return. This means that when I give God my worries, I get peace in return. Isaiah 61 testifies to the greatness of this very exchange. The promise is that He will give us...

Beauty for ashes.
Joy for mourning.
Praise for heaviness.

Obstacles are inevitable for all people no matter where they come from. In order to stay healthy, we must choose to see the obstacles with a perspective that says, 'This is happening for me, not to me.' We have to let go of the victim mentality in order to see that all obstacles are opportunities to expand our capacity to love and enjoy life.

Here is a helpful truth: in all of life you are either winning, or you are learning.

Each experience is either worth celebrating or worth listening to. If your relationship is going really well, that is a gift that should be celebrated and enjoyed. If your relationship is going poorly, it is an opportunity to learn why that is and how to make it better. If business is going well, that is worth celebrating and thanking God for. If it is not, it is an opportunity to ask God what is next and what you can learn from it.

No matter what is happening, life is teaching us something if only we will allow it to do so. The key is always going to be 'IF.' When we choose to come off autopilot and engage God in the midst of our circumstance, we will either give great thanks for the win or give Him space to teach us. James understood this well when he wrote this passage:

"Consider it all joy, my brothers and sisters, when you encounter various trials, knowing that the testing of your faith produces endurance. And let endurance have its perfect result so that you may be perfect and complete, lacking nothing."[4]

Did you catch that?

James said "when," not "if." James knew that trials are a normal part of life and that the invitation is whether or not we will consider them pure joy. Why? Because trials, obstacles, and problems teach us and grow us in the ways that we need, but that we may not step into voluntarily. These are the opportunities to deepen our root system and become the person that God created us to be. The curveballs are intended to free us from taking life too personally and make space for us to grow in Christ. Hence, the saying: 'you either get better or you get bitter,' meaning we either grow and learn, or we grumble and complain. We have trusted, then we have learned, and now we are able to give thanks.

THANKS

I have previously alluded to the fact that life has not been easy for me. I love my life, but that does not mean that it has always been an easy journey. Part of what has allowed me to have this view of life is a simple prayer that I pray often. The strength of this prayer is not in the words, but in the Person that I connect with in the words. The power is the way that I am reminded of what God is doing while I pray. The prayer goes something like this:

Thank you God for helping me understand that this problem has already been solved for me.

Give this a try right now.

Set your book down and take a few deep breaths.

Think about one of the problems that you are currently facing, and then pray this prayer slowly:

Thank you God for helping me understand that this problem has already been solved for me.

Prayer is powerful and there are many forms of prayers, from intercession to supplication to petition to declaration and more. This type of prayer is called a prayer of assurance. It is a time to be confident that God goes before us to prepare the way for us through the obstacles that we face. We are asking God to help us understand that the problems we face are already being solved by Him.

This week alone, as I write this, I have prayed this prayer about my car, a financial complication, a conversation/conflict with my wife about changing bedsheets (if you're married, you understand). When I pray this prayer, more often than not, nothing changes in my immediate circumstances. What does change is that I shift the weight of the problem from my shoulders to God's shoulders. The result of that shift is thanksgiving to God for all that He has done.

Thankfulness is a byproduct of something being done for us or given to us. When we pray prayers like this, we cultivate a lifestyle that understands that what we have has actually been given to us from God, which naturally leads to thanksgiving and gratitude. As we cultivate this kind of lifestyle, it allows us to face the hard parts of life from a redemptive, hopeful, and trusting heart through whatever we are facing.

ALL IS A GIFT

Getting comfortable with the uncomfortable is the only way through life's many twists and turns. But, this is only possible if we are able to frame the challenges and obstacles as opportunities, not setbacks. We must learn that each challenge is a chance to trust, to learn, and to give thanks. God is constantly extending the invitation to each of us to believe in Him and His ways, but this will mean taking the gaze off of ourselves and placing it back on Him. When we do this, we are able to see our lives as a small piece of a much larger puzzle, and that the picture that is being created is one of a restoration of the entire universe.[5]

It is a good day when we are convinced that God is making all things new, when we know a day is coming where there will be no more tears and no more pain. In the meantime, God wants to remind us that this life is a gift, and that we can stay tender through hard things knowing that in Him there is always a solution.

Today, let us step into a more robust prayer life, thanking Him for the breakthrough, the solution, and for knowing what to do.

CHAPTER 6 REFLECTION QUESTIONS

1. What stood out to you most from this chapter? Why do you think that is? How could you apply this?

2. In stressful or unforeseen circumstances do you naturally respond with fear & frustration, defeat & helplessness, or overwhelm & anxiety?

3. Which way of facing ourselves spoke to you most? Trust, Learn, or Thanks? Why do you think this is? How could this be applied to change how you respond to obstacles in the future?

CHAPTER 7: FREEDOM TIME

A GOD PROBLEM

It is no secret that comparison is running rampant in our world: we see it inside the church, we see it outside the church, we see it in successful CEOs, we see it in the young twenty-somethings. Theodore Roosevelt once said, "Comparison is the thief of joy." Not only does comparison steal away our happiness, it suffocates our souls. When we compare ourselves to others, it becomes difficult to appreciate our own lives and our own accomplishments. When we fill our minds with thoughts about what we lack, we create a never ending cycle of insignificance and insecurity. We simply are not wired for comparison.

At the root of comparison is a God problem. It is not something that can be fixed by trying harder or a problem that will hopefully disappear with age. Comparison is the fruit of our misunderstanding about who God is and confusion about who we are.

In order for us to be truly secure, we must tackle the problem at the source: we must understand how God sees us. When we don't feel secure in our relationship with God, it can be difficult to feel secure in our relationships with others. For some, this seems like an overnight process where God provides a revelation of divine love that instantly changes our perspective; for others, this will be a lifetime journey of discovering our identity as dearly loved children of God, who lack nothing in Him.[1]

A GOD SOLUTION

As we grow in intimacy with God, we continually learn that our significance and value comes from what He thinks about us, not what we do for Him. The more that we allow God's thoughts to influence us, the less concerned we become with how others think about us. I like to refer to this revelation as "The Lion King Moment."

When was the last time that you watched *The Lion King?*

If the answer is something to the affect of, "I don't know, I was probably a kid," then it is probably time to rewatch the film. Aside from being awesome, there is a deep revelation in this movie about the importance of understanding what the Father says about us. We see a young Simba, born the son of the king, but lost on his journey, unable to move forward after the unexpected death of his dad, Mufasa. Simba becomes confused about who he is apart from his dad, and at that moment the miraculous happens. That night, the sky opens above the water (which represents new birth), and Mufasa appears to remind Simba who he is and what he is called to be.

Sound familiar?

We are no different from Simba: sons and daughters who need to hear the voice of our Father telling us our truest identity and our truest calling.

The point is this: the way out of comparison is always a real connection to God and the voice of our Father.

God's voice reminds us who we are, regardless of whether or not others can see us that way. Even Jesus, who was literally God, needed the voice of the Father to remind Him of His true identity. This is the voice of Love, the voice that tells us who we are before we have even done a thing to earn approval. When we come to know and believe that we are the beloved of God, the healing power of God is released to the most broken parts of our soul. This is a truth that we can never graduate from, being *the beloved of God* (be-loved). This is a truth that we will need to remind ourselves of our entire lives. Learning to identify as the *beloved* is the key that sets us free to "be" and lets us out of the prison of comparison.

Until we are able to identify ourselves as who God says we are, we will always struggle with looking to the left and to the right to validate who we are. True freedom is knowing we are loved as we are in this very moment. There is no status, achievement, or personality trait that can be developed that will ever increase our worth and value in the eyes of God. Believing that we can work our way towards love is like running on a hamster wheel: a lot of energy is spent moving, but we are going absolutely nowhere.

Comparison, like rats to trash, feeds off of our insecurity and diverts our eyes from our true source of freedom. In walking with individuals from all walks of life, I am convinced we are ALL in the process of being convinced that God really loves us. The revelation of God's unconditional and always for you love is the path into deeper security than we could possibly experience anywhere else. Learning to be with God and hear His voice frees us from the trap of comparison. It allows us to lock eyes with the Person who loves us most, which means we don't need to be so concerned with what others are doing or how they react to us. When our eyes are on God, we can finally rest. We can finally step off the hamster wheel and enjoy the life God created us to live.

DESIGNED FOR LOVE

Comparison is a direct assault on our identity, attacking who we are and what we are made for. It attempts to blind us to our truest identity and calling. We must remember:

Each of us were created both *with* a purpose and *for* a purpose.

I believe that when we are not contributing to the flourishing of the world around us, we are actually "off" as humans. What I mean by this is that we were actually created to be a blessing in the world. We see this in Jesus' own life when He said, "My food is to do the will of Him who sent me, and to accomplish His work."[2] What Jesus is saying here is that doing the work that God prepared for Him was what energized Him each day. It was the source of energy for His body, soul, and spirit. As those made in His image, we are created no differently: we are designed to thrive when doing the work God has for us.

God designed us to live our life from His love. I often say that we live *from* love not *for* love. If we make working for God more important than being with God, we run into all sorts of issues. This is what we see in the story of Mary and Martha: Jesus affirming Mary's posture of someone wanting to listen to Jesus rather than Martha's posture of wanting to work for Jesus. We need to create the necessary space for Jesus to give us our true identity in order to move through life with delight and peace. If we want to love the people around us well, we must learn to prioritize being with God.

DON'T SHOULD YOURSELF

Being with God helps us to measure our lives accurately. Most people measure themselves against an ideal. They have created a version of themselves that they feel they should measure up to; however, that is not the version that they currently are. This means living in a constant state of not being good enough. This measurement is unhelpful to us because we are trying to hit a moving target. The ideal self that most of us create is an unrealistic version built on standards that almost always produce feelings of shame, inadequacy, and anxiety. This is very common in parents.

I am not sure I have met another parent who does not experience a low-grade, or even high-grade, shame for being a 'bad parent.' Oftentimes, this standard for 'good parenting' is based on an ideal picture of what a 'good parent' looks like, not against their own growth. This creates a cycle of shame where the parent is continually feeling defeated for their behavior, rather than excited about the growth they're experiencing with God. This is not exclusive to parents, it can apply to may different areas of life.

All of this behavior stems from a simple word: *should*.

You *should* call your parents each week, but you don't, so you feel like an inconsiderate child.

You *should* have known the perfect gift to get your spouse, but you didn't, and now you feel like you don't pay enough attention.

You *should* be reading your Bible each day, but you don't, and now you feel like God is upset with you.

Sound familiar? It is no wonder many sincere believers feel like crap as they live a life of "should-ing" all over themselves every day.

When our focus is on who we "should be" rather than appreciating where we are now, we are set up to experience disappointment, discontentment, and distress. Now, I know what you're thinking:

I don't really know how to just stop doing that. I would love to feel at peace with who I am and the journey I am on. It's just not that simple.

Here's the secret... it *is* that simple.

To experience an increased amount of peace in our lives, we simply need to change our measurement: rather than focusing on the ways we are not who we want to be, we begin to express gratitude for the growth and goodness that are happening now (if you would, please slowly reread that last sentence). This can be as simple as shifting the focus from what we feel is negative to a positive,

For example, instead of focusing on how you skipped bible reading in the week, you can thank God for the time that you spent in community, and moments you got to hear about the lives of the people around you.

Instead of remembering how you didn't get the perfect gift, you can highlight the time that you made your spouse feel loved by taking care of chores around the house.

Do you see the pattern?

Rather than put a magnifying glass over the things we could do better, we magnify the things that are working, the good things that are happening, and what God has put in our lives to bless us. We want to double down on the good and stop fixating on the negatives in our life. Sure, there will be moments when we could have done something differently; however, that doesn't mean that we shouldn't celebrate the awareness and desire we have for growth and change. Celebrating the good helps us to own our shortcomings while understanding that we are in forward motion.

It is so easy to stay stuck in the internal echo chamber of "I should be ________." Oftentimes, people spend far too much time "should-ing" when instead they could be celebrating about what God is doing in their lives. When we live measuring ourselves against the ideal-self we created (who we "should be"), we are often unconsciously hyper-focusing on areas of lack instead of appreciating the rich life we have been cultivating in God.

God intends for us to live lives full of rejoicing, prayer, and thankfulness. The discouragement that we feel when we are magnifying the negatives in our lives is a trick that can steal us from the life God intends for us. Paul understood this, which is why he reminded the church in Thessalonica to "Rejoice always, pray without ceasing; in everything give thanks; for this is God's will for you in Christ Jesus."[3]

In order to live a joyful life in God, we have to measure success the way that God does. This means looking at the whole story, not just a single sentence in our story. We have to measure our lives against where we have been and where we are today, not who we think we should be at this point in time. We need people around us who make a big deal of progress. These are the people who can come alongside us while we are in process and see who we really are in the Lord.

Let's think about one of those 'bad days.' You know, the type of day where you get home and think, 'I just want to eat and go to bed.' Rather than comparing how the day went with our perfect day, we can take a moment to reflect on what went well in that day. We can pause and ask God to show us what He wanted to teach us that day. We can fail-forward with Him and lean on our community to help us sift through the muck of our day and find gold in it. In all of life, we are either winning or learning. Tough days can be seen as learning days, opportunities to lean back into the arms of complete goodness and mercy.[4] These are chances to grow, and learn to see what is working instead of everything that isn't working.

THE BURDEN IS LIGHT

Learning to find the gold in life, whether that is in people, places, or seasons, is the secret to getting out of comparison in our life. Whether we are comparing ourselves to an ideal or to others, we have to learn a new way if we want to experience joy and peace in our lives.

Now, pause… we are almost there.

Before we end this section, I want to leave you with a friendly pastoral reminder.

Most of us are far too hard on ourselves. We are often overly critical of little thoughts and actions that don't align with the ideal person we want to be. As a friend of your journey, I want to tell you that this isn't helping you. When we partner with the negative, instead of lean into God's positives, we stay stuck and perpetuate a cycle of defeat. For many of us, we have way too high of expectations on ourselves. We make a lot of life high stakes when the reality is almost all of life is low stakes.

Learning to enjoy God each day and the unique journey we are on (with gratitude) is our onramp into true freedom that He has for each of us. Our time on this earth is simply a journey of discovering who God already says we are and doing what He has prepared for us to do.

Remember, God is doing a work in you that is going to lead to His glory and the good of the people around you. God has already said you are worth dying for and that your life is so precious He would give up His own just so you could live yours. Now it is time for you to begin discovering the same things He sees in you, empowering you to live out your God-ordained purpose on this earth.

More simply stated, as the Good Book puts its, "This is the day that the Lord has made; let us rejoice and be glad in it."[5]

CHAPTER 7 REFLECTION QUESTIONS

1. What stood out to you most from this chapter? Why do you think that is? How could you apply this?

2. Bring to mind an area where you feel you are not 'measuring up.' Who are you comparing to? Is it to an ideal version of yourself? Is it to another person? Once you've identified where you are comparing ask God what He thinks about that.

3. What is an area of life where you find that you tend to 'should' on yourself? How could you partner with the positives in this area instead of the negatives?

CHAPTER 8: GROWING CAPACITY

I want to wind us down with a really practical chapter. We will end this book with a compilation of ten helpful ways to grow our capacity. Growing our capacity is what helps us to successfully navigate challenges in life. As our capacity grows, so does the Kingdom, alongside our ability to love people well. We also become less prone to self-sabotaging and shutting down, allowing us to face hardships without giving up. Most importantly, growing our capacity helps to keep us tender towards Jesus as we continue on the journey of life.

In 1 Chronicles, Jabez boldly asks God not just for a blessing, but specifically for his territory to be enlarged. Jabez understood what many of us forget: the blessing grows alongside our capacity, as God blesses us, He will also stretch us. This stretching allows us to steward what we have been given without being overwhelmed. Without growing our capacity, we inevitably set ourselves up to live overwhelmed, living from our own strength rather than His Spirit-led strength.

If we do not intentionally grow our capacity as we journey through life, we end up plateauing. We play it safe. We protect ourselves. Our world gets smaller while God continues inviting us into more; however, we cannot carry the "more" without connection to God. When we lack connection to God, we are left with living from our own strength and our inner peace is volatile, depending on how we are feeling. However, when capacity is increased through connection, peace is maintained because we are staying connected to Peace Himself. We are able to respond to challenges with love because we are connected to Love. This increased capacity creates the space for deeper relationships, new opportunities, and greater appreciation of the life God has given us.

This list below of "capacity growers" is by no means exhaustive. However, I will say that each of them are guaranteed to increase what you can carry in life. We all have a threshold. There is only so much squeeze each of us can take on before we pop. The good news is that by keeping connection to God and giving thought to our ways, we can continue to enlarge our threshold for God's glory and the good of others.

CAPACITY GROWER 1: A YIELDED LIFE

In the Sermon on the Mount, Jesus reminds listeners of the need to be "poor in spirit." This reminder is an invitation to moment-by-moment dependence on God. When we live dependent (as Jesus did with the Father), we allow God to give us the power we need for all the things going on in our lives. This yielded way of living produces real joy and strength as we go through life.

Walking with God is not a math problem where we can simply arrive at a solution. It is much more like writing a story: we are immersed in the process, we gather new insights through the journey, and at the end, we are left with something to share with the world. Moment-by-moment surrender to God is what adds excitement, beauty, and meaning to our story. A life that values the thoughts, voice, and heart of God more than anything else is the kind of life that knows God and can't help glorify but God for who we know He is.

When we give our lives to God in this way, our capacity must expand so that we can handle all the opportunities that God has for us.

The opposite of a surrendered life is a 'white-knuckled life.' A 'white-knuckled life' happens when we try to control outcomes. When we spend our time trying to keep everything according to our plans and timelines, life becomes difficult. The question you can ask yourself to discover which life you are living is this:

Who or what am I most dependent on throughout the day?

Is it God? Is it others? Is it circumstances?

These questions, when answered honestly with God and others, are so helpful in helping us correct our course in life.

The posture of King David in Psalms 121 should encourage us when it comes to looking for help in life: "I lift up my eyes to the hills —where does my help come from? My help comes from the Lord, the Maker of heaven and earth."

The longer we walk with God, the more convinced we should become that our level of peace is in direct proportion to our surrender to the Spirit of God. A yielded life is a life of immense capacity. I love the way Paul said it, that when we yield our lives to God, something mystical happens to us: Jesus is able to live His life through us.[1]

CAPACITY GROWER 2: HARD QUESTIONS

Learning to ask "hard questions" is a very helpful way to increase capacity.

Questions have a way of going straight to our heart: the place where our emotions and motives live. When we take the time to ponder a question and answer honestly, we often discover motives, thoughts, or emotions that were sitting below the surface of our conscious thinking. Has this ever happened to you:

Someone asks you a question, and you answer it without really thinking. Later, you reflect more on the question and realize what your "real answer" is, and it is much more impactful than you realized?

That is the power of a well-positioned question.

Questions often shine a light on things that have been lurking in the shadows: corners we are cutting, pain we are avoiding, or mindsets that are setting us up for failure. Often when we make the space to reflect on hard questions with God, it is surprising what is revealed to us. We may remember a moment of anger in the day that we "brushed off," or maybe we recall a time where we rushed through something and weren't satisfied with what we did. Regardless, the questions that we ask help us to see ourselves and God more clearly.

It's helpful to consider how questions are used in scripture, so let me share some food for thought. First, after Adam and Eve are misled and disobey God, God addresses them with a question: "Where are you?" This question is God gently inviting Adam and Eve back into connection and removing unhealthy emotions like shame and guilt from their experience. Next, it is recorded that Jesus asked over 300 questions in His ministry. That is 300 questions in the Bible alone, not including the things He asked that didn't get written down. God often uses questions in order to empower us to engage in our own growth, while He walks alongside us to see things from a different perspective.

If you want to grow your capacity, asking yourself difficult questions is an easy way to level-up. Take time to ponder and write down your answers. Then consider handing someone else those same questions to ask you. Hearing yourself say your answers out loud is an even more effective way to level-up.

CAPACITY GROWER 3: FEEDBACK

One of my favorite books of the Bible is Proverbs. It is essentially a father passing down wisdom to his son about how to walk in righteousness, avoid pitfalls, and receive feedback. This is because receiving feedback is one of the quickest ways to grow our capacity in God; it is 'miracle grow' for the soil of our soul.

Many people resist feedback, often because of unhealthy examples in childhood that resulted in trauma. However, feedback is essential to helping us recognize our blindspots, the areas of weakness that aren't in our current vision. If we want to grow our capacity, we need to see the obstacles that are in the way of our maturity. Feedback provides a simple and clear way to get our attention to see the obstacles.

I'll be the first to say that I naturally resist feedback. I can't tell you how many times someone is correcting me, while internally I'm saying, "nope. nope. nope." However, the majority of the time, when I process this correction with the Lord, He reveals to me that many of the things said were spot on. Learning to stay open to both well-delivered feedback as well as the not-so-well delivered feedback is vital to our health in God.

Feedback requires humility, especially when it is unrequested. This is why I like to remind everyone that when receiving feedback, you can chew the meat and spit out the bones. This means that you can reflect on what was said, take what is helpful, and leave what is unhelpful behind. Remember, correction is not the same thing as rejection.

Correction is not the same thing as rejection.

The more we open ourselves up to correction, the easier it will be to grow our capacity in God. Remember, we are either winning or learning in life. Feedback is always an opportunity to learn and step into more growth if we welcome it instead of pushing it away.

CAPACITY GROWER 4: REFUSE TO BE OFFENDED

Have you ever had someone say something that didn't just attack your actions, but your character?

For most of us, this will happen many times throughout our lives and often it offends us. Learning to live with an unoffendable heart and not take life so personally will help keep us moving forward in life.

One of the hardest emotions for most people to experience is the feeling of being misunderstood. While this is by no means a fun feeling, it is something that is common and can actually grow our capacity if we learn to move through it.

One way to do so is to be convinced that God understands what we are going through, so we are never truly misunderstood. Let me invite you to read this again, slowly, while considering the gravity of what I am saying:

God understands what we are going through, so we are never misunderstood.

When we grasp the fact that God completely understands us, we are free from feelings of being misunderstood. This means that when we begin to feel offended, we no longer need to activate our inner lawyer, building a case to defend ourselves. Rather, we can rest, knowing that the God who made everything knows who we are and is a proud Dad.

In my almost twenty years of pastoring, I have experienced everything from betrayal, people being offended by who I am, being misunderstood more times than I can count, and even people believing and expressing that they can do a better job than me. Looking back, I can say that each moment was necessary for my growth and taught me the importance of going lower. I love to remind myself and people I mentor that water always finds the lowest place — that humility always wins. Jesus has abundant grace for those who go the lowest, especially when pride wants us to stay offended.

Jesus lived His life postured as a sacrificial lamb, knowing He was destined to be crucified. However, Jesus also lived knowing that the way of the lamb will always defeat the way of the dragon. Humility is always the path to truly winning in life. The invitation to follow Jesus will often lead us into moments that feel like death, but it is important to remember that you're in good company. When offense comes, the safest place to be is next to Jesus, a man who was more misunderstood than anyone else in history.

Offense is an invitation to increase capacity, teach us the way of the Lamb, and learn to love from a deeper place.

CAPACITY GROWER 5: GOD IS GOOD AND LIFE IS HARD

Throughout life, we are constantly battling for a correct view of God, a view that says, "God is good, only does good, and will always work all things for good." The reality that we must learn to accept is that God is good and life is hard until heaven comes to earth. Our capacity to enjoy all the blessings God has in store for us will either be set back or accelerated by our trust in His goodness.

King David said he would have despaired life if not for his belief in the goodness of God.[2] I don't know if we are very different, as the goodness of God is at the core of what allows us to move forward despite challenges. It is like a pair of glasses that allow us to see beauty and hope where we previously saw pain. There will be many obstacles that we face in life, but the promise is that all things are working for good. The key is that we know and believe that *all* things are working for good, not just most things or some things. Everything is being orchestrated for our good. This means the goodness of God is present all around:

Your losses are being used for good.
Your pain is being used for good.
Your mistakes are being used for good.
Your life, with the good, bad, and ugly, is being used for good.

God is the author of goodness in the world, not of evil. This fact can help us to trust the process, whether we currently understand what is happening or not. Confidence in the goodness of God allows us to grow our capacity because it tells us how things end up: good! This fact means that we can be confident that there is goodness coming our way, no matter the pain we face, the setbacks we experience, or the suffering we go through.

Our God is committed to acting only one way toward us in this life: good.

CAPACITY GROWER 6: CHOOSE TO BE A PRISONER OF HOPE

Expectancy can be a great way to increase our capacity.

When we live our lives expecting good things to happen, it is actually easier to endure the moments of disappointment or pain that inevitably come.

In the same way that a runner can increase their lung capacity, making running easier, we can increase our expectancy so that we can go further in the journey of life. One of the easiest ways to grow our expectancy is to find the good things happening around us and celebrate them. Whenever we reflect and spend intentional time giving thanks to God for the good in our life, we are increasing that expectancy. It is like we are working out our "joy muscles," leading to greater hope for the future.

My favorite definition of hope is 'a positive expectation of God's goodness in every circumstance and situation.'

Reflect on that for a moment.

Hope is a positive expectation of God's goodness in every circumstance and situation.

Think about your own life now.

Do you believe that God's goodness is headed your way at this moment?

This question can easily serve as a way to measure whether you are believing in the truth of who God is, or partnering with lies that are trying to steal your hope. If you find that you are not believing that God's goodness is coming toward you, then it is important to train yourself to see the goodness around you.

We are all able to train ourselves in this way. Those who have trained themselves to see the good that God is doing are able to celebrate Him everywhere: the sunrise and sunset, a good cup of coffee, time with a friend, or simply the sound of a chirping bird outside. These simple parts of life are all reminders of God's goodness. The more that we celebrate these wins, the easier they become to recognize. The more that we can recognize them, the more that we expect them. The more that we expect them, the greater our capacity grows.

The prophet Zechariah encourages us to choose this day to be a prisoner of Hope: "Return to your stronghold, O prisoners of hope; today I declare that I will restore to you double."[3]

CAPACITY GROWER 7: LIFE IS ABOUT RELATIONSHIPS

If we miss this, then we miss everything.

Life is about God and people.

God calls us to be relational before we are ever called to be functional. What I mean by this is that the people around us are far more important than what we accomplish in our lives. This is why Jesus emphasized the importance of solving issues within relationships before we go commune with Him.[4] He clearly understood that our horizontal relationship would affect our vertical relationship.

If we want to keep our hearts tender towards God, then we must make relationships the end, not the means. We must seek to live with a good conscience not just before God, but also before all people at all times.[5]

Learning to fight for the health of relationships and to see people as God sees them is a never ending journey. As we know, the problem is that oftentimes people are difficult to love. In order to love people well, we need to treat them based on who they are, not how they are acting towards us. We need to see others as people made in the image of God, who God was willing to die for, not as problems needing to be solved.

Much of our culture has lost sight of the value of people. To grow our capacity, we will need to set our focus on each person's value. When we do this, we inevitably end up loving people instead of using people.

It is only through seeing people with love, the same way God sees them, that we can grow our capacity and step into what God is inviting us into.

CAPACITY GROWER 8: SILENCE

In regards to growing capacity, I don't know of a more fruitful spiritual practice than silence. The practice of spending time simply sitting before

God can do more for the inner world than just about anything else I can think of. Silence has an underestimated ability to produce freedom in us: freedom from unhealthy attachment, freedom from impulse living, and freedom from performance, just to name a few.

Blaise Pascal insightfully noted, "All of humanity's problems stem from man's inability to sit quietly in a room alone."

This quote constantly reminds me of the importance of sitting before the Lord, of the importance of being patient and still. We need to take time to just "be" instead of always trying to "do." Often we relate to God through accomplishment: we read scripture, we intercede, we serve, etc. What I have found is that, more often than not, God just wants to spend time with us.

A good dad wouldn't only give time to their children after they have accomplished something. Wouldn't it be strange to see a parent who only spent time with their kid after all their school work and chores were done? Stillness is a place of connection. Stillness is where we can grow our capacity for peace, love, and awareness of God. Stillness brings awe of God and childlike wonder back into our lives.

I have noticed that the transforming work of silence is best measured in years, if not decades. The benefits cannot be evaluated in the short term. Oftentimes, we are unaware of what God is doing and how He is working in the moments that we are sitting with Him. However, the Word says that one of the guaranteed paths to transformation is beholding who God is. It is in this process of beholding that we are able to grow our capacity to receive more of who God is and the goodness that He has in store for us.[6]

CAPACITY GROWER 9: NEW CHALLENGES

"Christian" is an adventure word.

The problem is that many of us treat being a christian like a noun (something we are) instead of a verb (something we do).

Oftentimes, people treat life with God as if it is something easy and repeatable, when in reality, it is an adventure that invites us into newness constantly. In order to grow our capacity, we need new cliffs to jump off of that require us to trust God more than we trust ourselves. This act of trust is what is often referred to as faith.

Faith is a muscle, which means it must be exercised or it will atrophy. This is what happens when we "cruise" in life.

I know that it may seem helpful to have a smooth path through life, but the opposite is actually true. We need the challenges, the difficulties, and the oppositions in order to grow best. We are more like palm trees than flowers. Palm trees grow best in the wind, they adapt and change with their environment, and they grow to be tall and fruitful. Flowers grow best when the soil is rich and the environment is easy, and many times, need to be replanted. New challenges, opportunities, and moments of discomfort actually help us to grow our capacity, not diminish it.

Never forget: courage is what God gives us when we face our fear.

Courage is what Joshua needed to face the giants that were blocking the promised land. Courage is what David needed to go up against Goliath.

Courage is what Jesus needed to go to the cross. Courage is what God gives us to face the things that are standing in the way of the blessing.

For most people, fear is what inhibits us from stepping into the good things God has prepared for us. We fear the unknown, even though God has an open door for us. As I heard a pastor once say, "The dogs of doom stand at the doors of destiny." Often the places where we feel the most fear are actually the areas where we are stepping more into the incredible life God has for us. I believe that just about anything that we are destined for will have fear blocking the way. It is our choice to depend on God and continue to move forward through the fear.

We must remember that there is always a new opportunity on the other side of fear. May we not forget that our enemy loves fear; God, however, loves faith. This is why stepping out of our comfort zone is always guaranteed to grow our capacity. Growth occurs when we are faced with the unfamiliar and the uncomfortable. Taking these opportunities with God and trusting that He will provide courage is what grows our capacity for more of His goodness in our lives.

CAPACITY GROWER 10: JUST SAY NO

If we want to love well, we need to have love to give. We simply cannot give what we do not have. Now, I am not saying that God cannot give us increased capacity to do work when we feel empty (welcome to parenting 101). However, I am saying that stewarding our capacity allows for greater health both for us and the people around us. In order to do this, we have to get very good at saying a very simple word: No.

In the western world, we can have almost anything we want, at any time we want. Despite this, many are unsatisfied. This is because our deepest desires, satisfaction, and longings have never been outside of us, but instead are inside of us.

In the fourth century AD, Saint Augustine of Hippo said "You have made us for Yourself, and our hearts are restless until they find rest in You.'

When we feel restless, we often grasp for something to relieve us instead of to restore us. To be relieved, we simply experience a momentary reduction of pain and discomfort, or we experience a momentary increase in pleasure of comfort. This is why many people turn to destructive habits such as alcohol or scrolling or other forms of addiction. However, what we are really looking for is restoration.

Restoration is returning to an original or desired state. For the people of God, this is a soul-level return to the life God intended, the life presented in the Garden of Eden. This is life where we are deeply in-tune with God, walk with God, and aren't burdened by the pressures of life. This kind of life allows our soul to soar and our bodies to flourish.

When we are living in a constant state of finding relief rather than restoration, it drains us of who we are and limits our capacity for what we can handle each day. If we want to live a "garden life," then we have to get good at finding restoration instead of relief. This requires saying "no" to the easy things in life.

Many people discover this when they hit rock bottom, but the lesson is available to you right now: no status, no place, no experience, and no person can ever bring the restoration that our souls crave. We are created for family, for relationship, and for something bigger than ourselves; however, if God is not at the center of that search, it will lead to pain. If God is at the center of this search, the promise is beauty and life. It may not be an easy life; however, it will be a life that echoes into eternity.

FINAL THOUGHTS

I pray this prayer from Ephesians often, whether it is over myself, my family, my friends, or the church: "May God give you a spirit of wisdom and of revelation in the knowledge of Him."[7] The secret to saying "no" to the easy way in life is a revelation of who God is. This is what I want to leave us all with as we end. All the truths in this book are helpful, but without a revelation of who God is, we are aiming for the wrong things. Let us remember, what we think about God really is what affects our lives more than any other thing.

By the grace of God, may we keep our eyes on the prize, run this race with integrity, and get good at bouncing back.

The grace to change is available each day, enabling us to live well and be able to join the

Apostle Paul at the end of our life saying what he said at the end of his life:

"I have fought the good fight, I have finished the course, I have kept the faith."[8]

CHAPTER 8 REFLECTION QUESTIONS

1. What stood out to you most from this chapter? Why do you think that is? How could you apply this?

2. Which of these capacity growers sound most challenging? Which sounds easiest to implement in your life?

3. How could you practice one or more of these capacity growers in this current season of life?

WHERE TO GO FROM HERE

First off, thank you for reading this book, for doing the work to grow, and for staying open to change. I have found that most people want to see a healthier and happier self, but often don't want to do anything different to see that happened.

The Good Book reminds us that the blessing is always on those who "do" what they are hearing, not on those who are only acquiring more information. When writing this book, I hoped that you wouldn't just learn more about God, but you would feel equipped to do life *with* God.

Now a few really practical suggestions...

- To get the most out of anything in life, we are best when doing it with other people. If you went through this book alone, consider re-reading with at least one other person, challenging each other with questions, and most importantly, discussing how to apply it.

- This book was meant to be eaten and digested slowly. A wise older man once told me that it is better to read a good book 10 times than 10 books once. I would apply this same thought process to certain chapters. One chapter may speak louder than another due to the season of life you are in. If that is the case, don't hesitate to post up a tent and stay in that chapter until you feel like you have mined the gold you needed out of it.

- Consider meeting up with a younger believer and go through the entire book together. A chapter a week with two simple questions: what spoke to you? how are you applying it? I have found that I learn differently when I feel a responsibility to know or teach the information.

- Lastly, feel free to email one or two of your biggest takeaways from reading the book. This would be a win-win with you taking time to reflect, process, and write out your response. And we woulds be blessed / love to hear how God used this book in your life: jasonlomelino@gmail.com

We pray that you will experience more of God in this next season of life, and that you continue to step into greater joy and health.

"And we proclaim Him, admonishing every man and teaching every man with all wisdom, that we may present every man mature in Christ. And for this purpose also I labor, striving according to His power, which mightily works within me." (Colossians 1:28-29).

All is grace,
Jason & Ryland

INDEX

CHAPTER 1

1. James 4:2-3
2. John 10:10
3. Psalms 139:23-24

CHAPTER 2

1. John 14:26 & 1 John 2:27
2. 2 Timothy 3:16-17
3. Psalms 139:3

CHAPTER 4

1. Romans 12:1-2
2. 2 Corinthians 3:18
3. *The Knowledge of the Holy* by A.W. Tozer

CHAPTER 6

1. 1 John 4:18
2. Proverbs 31:25
3. Isaiah 53:3
4. James 1:2-4
5. 2 Corinthians 5:19

CHAPTER 7

1. Psalms 23:1
2. John 4:34
3. 1 Thessalonians 5:16-17
4. Psalms 23:6
5. Psalms 118:24

CHAPTER 8

1. Galatians 2:20
2. Psalms 27:13-14
3. Zechariah 9:12
4. Matthew 5:23
5. Acts 24:16
6. 2 Corinthians 3:18
7. Ephesians 1:17
8. 2 Timothy 4:7

JESUS BURGERS, VOLUME 1: The story of Jesus Burgers is told through over twenty people whose lives were transformed through this ministry in Isla Vista, California, an infamous party town adjacent to the University of California, Santa Barbara. Isla Vista Church, a family of believers, have gathered weekly to serve burgers and the love of Jesus to the hundreds of partiers for over a decade. The city has come to know and appreciate this ministry and the many transformed lives.The success of Jesus Burgers is spreading, inspiring other college campus ministries across the country to launch their own Jesus Burgers outreach ministries. This is the Jesus Burgers story.

A LIFE THAT WINS: WHAT DOES IT MEAN TO WIN AT LIFE? Who is depositing seeds today to grow the fruit trees of tomorrow? Who is intentionally living present in life instead of busily living for the next "like" on social media? The answer is WINNERS. We must develop mindsets that will produce the fruit of the life we were designed to live. Everyone was meant to win at life; we actually were created to win. In the eyes of God, there aren't any losers, only winners. However, it is what we choose to do each day, both in thought and action, that allows us to step into rhythms and a lifestyle that wins.

60-DAY CHALLENGE: This book is written for those who want to grow in Christ and cultivate healthy rhythms in life. In saying "yes" to this book (for the next 60 days), you are agreeing to go on a journey that is guaranteed to upgrade your life in God and help you live in the awareness of His presence more and more each day. I have intentionally made this book as simple as possible, for all ages, and walks of life - those who have walked with Jesus for 50 years and those who have known Him for 5 days. Anyone and everyone can pick this book up, make sense of it, and use it as a springboard to know God more.

60-DAY DISCIPLESHIP: This book is written for those who want to grow in Christ and cultivate healthy rhythms in life. In saying "yes" to this book (for the next 60 days), you are agreeing to go on a journey that is guaranteed to upgrade your life in God and help you live in the awareness of His presence more and more each day. I have intentionally made this book as simple as possible for all ages, and walks of life — those who have walked with Jesus for 50 years and those who have known Him for 5 days. Anyone and everyone can pick this book up, make sense of it, and use it as a springboard to know God more.